A
year in my
kitchen

PHOTOGRAPHY BY
Jason Lowe

A year in my kitchen

SKYE GYNGELL

TEN SPEED PRESS
Berkeley

Published in the United States by Ten Speed
Press, an imprint of the Crown Publishing
Group, a division of Random House, Inc.,
New York.
www.crownpublishing.com
www.tenspeed.com

Ten Speed Press and the Ten Speed Press
colophon are registered trademarks of
Random House, Inc.

Originally published in hardcover in Great
Britain by Quadrille Publishing Limited,
London, in 2006.

Library of Congress Cataloging-in-
Publication Data on file with publisher

ISBN 978-1-58008-052-1
Printed in China

Publishing director: Jane O'Shea
Creative director: Helen Lewis
Project editor: Janet Illsley
Art direction and design: Lawrence Morton
Photographer: Jason Lowe
Stylist: Cynthia Inions
Production: Bridget Fish

notes

Please use sea salt, freshly ground pepper,
and fresh herbs (except in the rare instances
where I have specified dried herbs).

I use medium organic eggs. Anyone who is
pregnant or in a vulnerable health group
should avoid recipes using raw egg whites
or lightly cooked eggs.

10 9 8 7 6 5 4 3 2 1
First U.S. Edition

Introduction

Fresh, ripe, seasonal ingredients are at the core of my cooking. There is a wonderful sense of anticipation, as well as a comforting familiarity, if you cook with the seasons. For instance, knowing that sweet, juicy damsons will be here for their short two-week stay around mid-September, or that the complex flavor of blood oranges will bring a warm glow to the barren winter months of January and February is deeply reassuring.

It is June as I write and the first cherries are making their short appearance—bringing with them happy childhood memories. Come fall, wild hazelnuts will be available and beautiful walnuts arrive from Périgord. Cooking with the seasons provides a sense of life's continuity—a feeling that everything is just right with the world ... an ease with ingredients naturally follows.

At the nursery, we source ingredients as locally as possible and I urge you to do the same. Seek out quality suppliers, ideally supporting your local grocer, fish supplier, butcher, and/or farmers' market. It is a good way to learn more about the food you are eating and helps you to make a connection with the earth, seasons, environment, and the people around you. I find it impossible to make that connection through grocery shopping alone.

Good food begins with good ingredients, carefully sourced and at their seasonal best, but what really makes a good cook? Certainly, it has to do with practice and accumulated experience. As with any skill, the more frequently it is performed, the more confidence and knowledge will be gained. It is also important to begin to understand the rationale behind certain techniques—to appreciate what you are doing and why.

However, it is perhaps even more crucial to develop a feel and an intuition for food and cooking. Then heart, hands, and head work together to produce something worthwhile.

A recipe is simply a documentation of a cooking process. Its function is to provide a list of ingredients and an idea of the method and structure of a dish, which is invaluable to the inexperienced cook. But merely following a recipe is ultimately an unfulfilling experience, unless you learn to apply all your senses—taste and sight, of course, but also smell, touch, and emotion. Only then will you begin to understand the very nature of the dish.

Ask yourself

questions about produce before you buy: "Where does it come from?" "Is it fresh?" "In season?" "Grown locally?" "Does it really inspire me to cook?" "Does its very appearance make me hungry?"

Tasting food

as you cook is very important. To rest assured that a dish will be fine because you have followed a recipe is an incorrect assumption. Taste, pause, and consider what the dish needs. More often than not, it will be attention to seasoning, or perhaps a little lemon zest or minced parsley to clean up the flavors ... or possibly nothing at all!

I don't see food as a work of art. Certainly, thought and composition are important. Food on a plate should appeal to the eye as well as the palate, but never at the expense of flavor. When clever technique and fragile structures are all that are considered, a dish will live only for a short time in the memory.

My greatest learning experience in the last few years has been working with a kitchen garden. At Petersham, our garden is modest, but it has provided me with a direct and immediate appreciation of the seasons, as well as an awe-inspiring respect for the richness of the earth. I have learned to feel a deep respect for the abundance that nature provides.

Food only ever really sings if you have put your heart and soul into it. Taste as you go along and feel free to put your own stamp on a dish—I cook what I feel is right.

For me, to cook is the most natural thing in the world. To work professionally as a chef can be very demanding, exhausting, and incredibly stressful—probably one of the least glamorous jobs for a woman! Yet I love it today as much as when I first started and I still dream about food when I sleep! I can't think of anything more exciting than to welcome in the new season's ingredients.

Above all, for me, cooking is an act of love and giving. It is about breaking bread with family and friends, about conviviality, and shared experience. As you glance through this book, I wish that you may begin to feel a little of the joy and deep sense of fulfillment that cooking has brought to my life. I sincerely hope that if you've not yet experienced the joy of cooking, it is waiting for you just around the corner.

Happy cooking!

A love of eating and a real appreciation of great produce—combined with a generosity of spirit and the desire to share with others—is at the core of beautiful food.

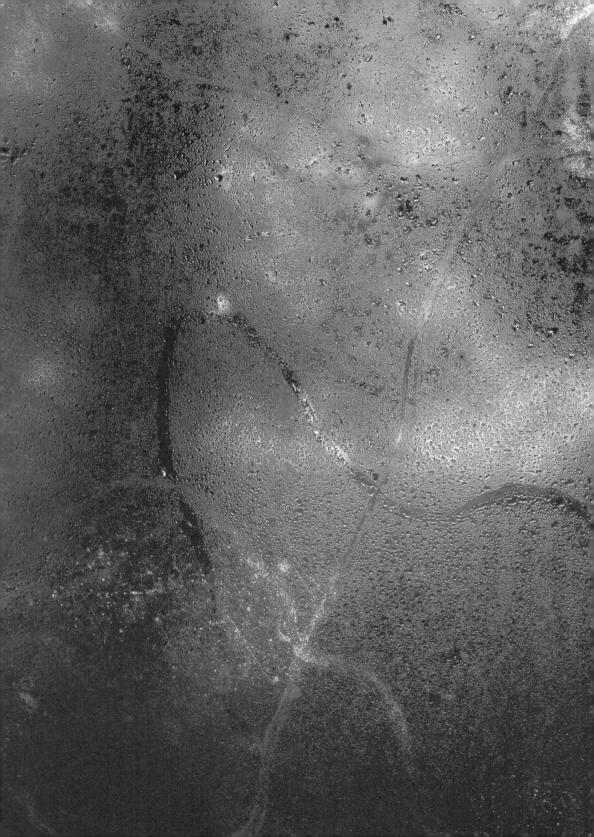

MY TOOLBOX

The toolbox is the "nuts and bolts" of my cooking. As the seasons change and new ingredients present themselves, it is the toolbox I turn to for inspiration. Over the years, I have found that these tools enable me to bring out the full natural flavors of seasonal ingredients and inspire me to create new dishes.

Every item in the toolbox works as a component to be added to something else—the "tools" act as conductors or enhancers of flavor and they come alive when they are added to another dish. They work without masking or overpowering the ingredients that I most want to highlight in a dish. Ultimately, they help me to achieve the balancing of flavors that is so critical to the way I cook. This toolbox really works for me and I hope it will for you too.

SKY

top note herbs

lemon zest

infused oils*

basil oil

vinaigrettes

mayonnaise bases

flavored yogurts

agrodolce

roasted red onions

slow-roasted tomatoes

toasted nuts

sourdough bread crumbs

braised lentils

tea-smoking

stock

roasted spice mix

base note herbs

EARTH

Base notes & top notes

In every dish that I cook, I am looking for the purest possible taste—an entirety. I think of it like the notes of the scale—beginning with the earthy base note flavors and finishing with the top notes that add freshness and make the dish "sing."

In the way that I cook, I am constantly seeking harmony—a balance of sweet, sour, and salty tastes. This isn't a new concept, it is the way people have cooked in the East forever.

* *chile, garlic, lemon-infused*

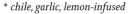

Base note herbs

I cannot imagine cooking without herbs, as I find them so essential to the taste of food. Base note herbs are the ones that help lay the foundations of a dish. They include bay, thyme, rosemary, sage, summer savory, and lovage. Parsley, when added to bay and thyme, forms the trinity that we call a bouquet garni, which is an essential part of soups, stocks, and slow-cooked dishes. Base note herbs endure the burden of long, slow cooking incredibly well, continuing to add their flavor as long as they are cooking.

Fresh herbs in season lend dishes an exceptional vibrancy and freshness. I think that dried herbs (possibly with the exception of mint) are not worth using—they only contribute a musty staleness to a dish.

Roasted spice mix

I use this combination of spices a great deal, because their flavors work particularly well together, lending a depth and sensory aroma to many purées and slow-cooked dishes. They definitely belong at the earth end of the scale and must be used in conjunction with other flavors in order to balance and pad them out. The spice mix is a foundation that only really works if the heat of chile is added, plus the sweetness of jaggery or maple syrup, and the sourness of tamarind, lemon, or lime. The saltiness of soy or fish sauce is also needed to underpin the spice mix flavor.

Buy whole spices for this—ready-ground spices will already have lost their freshness and give dishes a dull, musty taste. And for optimum flavor, use a mortar and pestle or spice grinder rather than a food processor to grind the mix. You can keep the roasted spice mix in a sealed container for up to a month, but no longer.

for the roasted spice mix

1 or 2 cinnamon sticks
2 ounces coriander seeds
2 ounces cumin seeds
2 ounces fennel seeds
2 ounces mustard seeds
2 ounces fenugreek seeds
5 cardamom pods
2 or 3 star anise (or cloves)

Place a dry, heavy skillet (preferably nonstick) over low heat. Break the cinnamon stick in half. Once a clear smoke begins to rise from your skillet, add all the spices and cook, stirring frequently, to toast them. Be careful not to burn them, though, as this would give a bitter taste. Once the seeds begin to pop, they are ready. Remove from the heat and grind to a fine powder. Store in an airtight container until ready to use.

Stock

The making of a good stock is an important foundation in cookery and one of the first things you learn as a young chef. In my mind, a stock cube is not a viable substitute—its flavor is essentially artificial and unpalatable when the stock is reduced down.

I have seen all sorts of things thrown into stocks as they are made—even red bell peppers, garlic, and vegetable peelings. I am totally against these additions. Because a stock acts as a building block, it needs to have a very pure base flavor. Other flavors only cloud and confuse the taste. Another rule when making a stock is to avoid adding salt. This is so that the stock can be reduced without it becoming too salty.

I use chicken stock for a wide range of dishes, but you can adapt this recipe if veal, beef, or lamb stock is more appropriate to the dish, simply by substituting the bones. Veal bones, in particular, make a lovely stock.

for the chicken stock

4 1/2 pounds chicken bones
3 yellow onions, peeled
6 carrots, peeled
3 celery stalks
olive oil
20 black peppercorns
4 bay leaves
small bunch of thyme
bunch of curly or Italian parsley
4 quarts water

Preheat the oven to 425°F (convection oven to 400°F). Lay the chicken bones in a large baking sheet and roast on the top shelf of the oven until golden brown, 12 to 15 minutes. Meanwhile, roughly chop the onions, carrots, and celery and place in a large stockpot or pan. Add the tiniest amount of olive oil and sweat over low heat until the vegetables soften slightly and start to release their flavors.

When the bones are nicely colored, add them to the vegetables along with the black peppercorns, bay leaves, thyme, and parsley. Pour in the water and bring just to a boil. Immediately turn down the heat to low and cook gently for 1 1/2 hours, skimming the scum from the surface every now and then. It is very important that a stock does not boil, as this causes the impurities to be dragged back down into the stock rather than collect on the surface where they can be removed.

At the end of the cooking time, you should have a pure, clean-tasting stock. Remove from the heat and strain through a fine strainer. Use as required. If preparing ahead, cool and refrigerate for up to 3 days, or freeze until needed.

Tea-smoking

I first came across this way of infusing flavor into food in Australia. The technique is best applied to oily fish, such as trout, wild salmon, or mackerel; it also works well with quail and chicken. You can experiment with any type of tea you like. I use Lapsang, Yunnan, and Earl Grey because they all have a very fragrant quality, which imparts a delicate, aromatic flavor to the fish or meat.

You will also need a large sturdy baking pan with a tight-fitting lid, a wire cake-cooling rack that will fit comfortably inside the baking pan, and four small metal heatproof bowls to hold the wire rack in place. A good exhaust fan is also handy as the smoking itself can impart a strong aroma ... albeit delicious!

for the tea-smoking mixture

1/4 cup packed light brown sugar
1/3 cup superfine sugar
4 1/2 ounces tea leaves

Shape 2 small cups from sturdy foil, 2 3/4 to 3 1/4 inches across the top and 3/4 to 1 1/4 inches deep. Mix the sugars and tea leaves in a bowl, then tip half this dry mixture into each foil cup and stand them in a baking pan, toward the middle. Position the 4 heatproof bowls in the corners of the pan and balance the wire rack on top.

Now cut parchment paper in the shape of the food you are tea-smoking. Lay the paper on the wire rack and place the food on top. Turn on your exhaust fan. Place the baking pan with the lid on top over medium-high heat (you will most likely need to place it across two burners).

It will take about 10 minutes for the smoke to get going and start to flavor the food. The cooking time depends on what you are smoking and whether you are cooking it completely or only partially. Refer to specific recipes for cooking times.

Braised lentils

I rarely choose to combine protein with carbs; for me, the mix is usually too heavy. However, I do like to work with legumes, especially lentils. Scattered over a dish, their earthy flavor and texture lend a real depth without detracting or masking the flavors of the other ingredients. The little brown Castelluccio lentils from Umbria in Italy are my favorite. Puy lentils are also very good and may be easier for you to find. You need to be careful not to overcook lentils or they will become sludgy—they need to retain a definite bite.

for the lentils

2¹/2 cups Castelluccio or Puy lentils

1 red or yellow onion, peeled and quartered

1 carrot, peeled and cut into 3 chunks

1 fresh red chile

2 cloves garlic, peeled

3/4 to 1¹/4-inch piece fresh gingerroot, peeled and roughly chopped

5 thyme or parsley sprigs

2 bay leaves

1 tbsp chopped cilantro root

2 tbsp sherry vinegar

2 tbsp tamari or soy sauce

2 tbsp sesame or walnut oil

Rinse the lentils and place them in a deep pan along with the onion, carrot, chile, garlic, ginger, thyme, bay leaves, and cilantro. Add enough water to cover the lentils completely and bring to a boil over medium heat. Lower the heat and simmer until the lentils are cooked but still have a bite, about 20 minutes.

Immediately remove from the heat and drain in a colander, then tip the lentils into a bowl. While they are still warm (so they absorb the flavors better), dress with the vinegar, tamari, and your chosen oil. Use as required.

You can keep these lentils in the refrigerator for up to 5 days, but take them out at least an hour before serving, to bring them back to room temperature.

Sourdough bread crumbs

I use these all the time—to add color and texture to food. I am drawn to sourdough breads because of their earthy, slightly fermented taste and wonderful chewy texture. Their crunchy, slightly rough bread crumbs give many dishes a really strong character. I sprinkle them over salads and warm dishes, and incorporate them into several sauce bases. As a toolbox item, they work in the same way as toasted nuts and braised lentils.

for the sourdough bread crumbs

1/2 loaf of good-quality sourdough

1/2 cup olive oil

sea salt and freshly ground black pepper

Preheat the oven to 400°F (convection oven to 375°F). Tear the bread into large chunks, leaving on the crust, then place in a food processor and pulse until you have rough bread crumbs. Tip into a bowl, add the olive oil, season with salt and pepper, and toss to mix.

Tip the bread crumbs onto a baking sheet and spread them out— they need to be well spaced to toast evenly. Place in the oven until golden and crunchy, 12 to 15 minutes, checking regularly and shaking the tray as you do so, to ensure the crumbs toast evenly.

Let the bread crumbs cool before using. You can store them in an airtight container for a week or so—they keep well as long as the air doesn't get to them.

Toasted nuts

Nuts lend texture and flavor, giving dishes a rustic quality that I find irresistible. Many are at their peak in the fall, the season when English cobnuts, a variety of hazelnuts, become available and French walnuts arrive from Périgord. I use good-quality nut oils too, preferably cold-pressed, as these are more subtle than toasted or heated nut oils.

Apart from scattering toasted nuts onto dishes, I also use them in sauces, such as the one I make using walnuts, anchovy, garlic, and sourdough bread crumbs to serve with broiled veal chops or roasted white fish. Another favorite is the Spanish sauce, Romesco—a pungent rough-textured mix of toasted almonds, dried roasted chiles, garlic, and virgin olive oil. I also use ground toasted almonds to thicken some dishes, such as fish and chicken stews.

Freshness is of the utmost importance. Buy nuts in their shells if you can and use them soon after purchasing, as they turn rancid fairly quickly. Nuts in shells need air, so they should be turned, while shelled nuts should be kept in an airtight container in a cool, dark cupboard.

Nuts, like spices, need to be gently warmed through before you use them, in order to release their flavor. There is no specific method to this and individual recipes will tell you how to prepare them. But, as a general guide, you can spread the nuts out on a baking sheet and put them in a preheated oven at 375°F (convection oven at 350°F) to warm and release their flavor, 3 to 4 minutes, or allow a little longer for a deeper color.

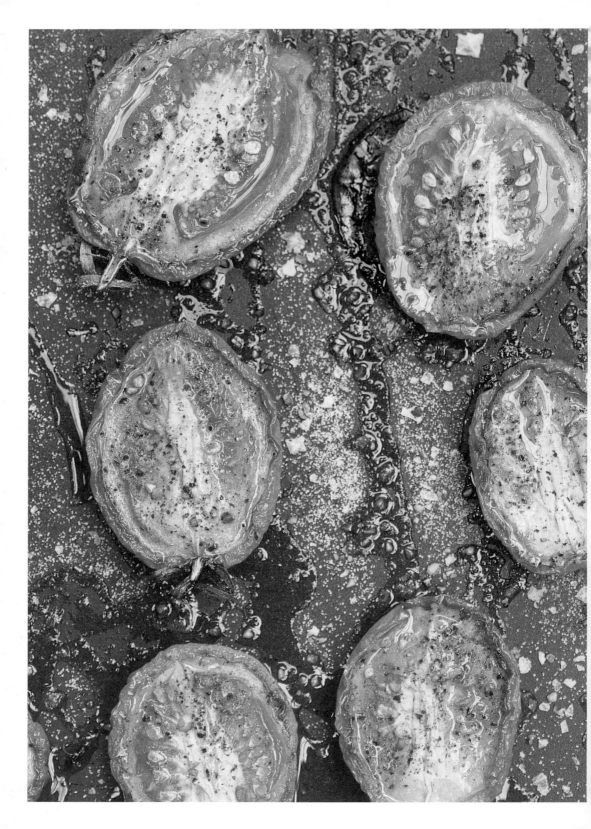

Roasted red onions

These beautiful, deep-purple rings lend a superb depth of flavor and color to many cold dishes. Their sharp sweetness sits somewhere in the middle of the scale. *Illustrated on previous spread.*

for the roasted onions

5 medium red onions, peeled

1/2 cup superfine sugar

sea salt and freshly ground black pepper

generous 3/4 cup balsamic vinegar

1/4 cup extra virgin olive oil

Preheat the oven to 375°F (convection oven to 350°F). Slice the onions into pinwheels, about 1/8 inch thick, and spread out on a large baking sheet. Sprinkle with the sugar and a generous pinch each of salt and pepper. Pour over the balsamic vinegar and olive oil and mix together lightly with your hands. Roast in the oven for 25 to 30 minutes, turning them (with tongs or a wooden spoon) and basting halfway through cooking. When the onions are ready, they should be deep purple in color and glistening, tasting sweet and sharp at the same time.

Slow-roasted tomatoes

These lend flavor and sweetness to many recipes and I have endless uses for them. Softer and less chewy than sun-dried tomatoes, they work really well with vegetables, fish, and red meat, and with cheeses, especially goat cheeses and ricotta. Warm from the oven, they are delicious with scrambled eggs on toast. They also form the basis of my Tomato and Chile Jam (page 32). I suggest you use plum tomatoes, as they have a good flavor and a pretty shape when semidried in this way (San Marzano is an excellent variety). It is important that they are ripe and in good condition. These slow-roasted tomatoes keep well for several days, or you can store them for longer (up to a month) in sterilized jars, kept covered with a layer of extra virgin olive oil.

for the slow-roasted tomatoes

6 plum tomatoes, halved lengthwise

1 tbsp superfine sugar

1/4 ounce sea salt

1/4 ounce freshly ground black pepper

Turn your oven on to its lowest possible setting—probably 250°F (convection oven to 225°F). Lay the tomatoes, cut side up, in a single layer on a large baking sheet. In a small bowl, mix together the sugar, salt, and pepper, then sprinkle all over the cut surface of the tomatoes. Roast, undisturbed, in the oven for 3 to 4 hours, until they shrivel up—their pointy ends turning up like Turkish slippers. Remove and set aside until ready to use. Slow-roasting intensifies the flavor, giving the tomatoes a deliciously sweet, earthy taste.

Agrodolce

The principle of agrodolce is essentially about achieving balance and harmony from contrasting tastes—salty (or savory) and sweet pulling against each other, yet complementing each other completely. It belongs in the toolbox because it is a concept that I love and one I find myself using time and time again.

You will come across agrodolce in most of my recipes, using the balance of tamari and maple syrup, or fish sauce and jaggery, or pickled fruits and salty pungent cheeses like feta, or young lemony goat cheese with tomato and chile jam or pickled figs, for example.

It takes a while to perfect the principle. Like a set of old-fashioned scales, the ideal balance lies in the middle, yet it takes very little (in the way of sweet or salty) to tilt it out of kilter in either direction. When it is well achieved, agrodolce creates a strong, clear, harmonious flavor that is deeply satisfying—notably in slow-cooked dishes, like Lamb with Prunes, Chile, Cilantro, and Spice Mix (page 180). The relishes on the following pages use the agrodolce principle to perfection.

Tomato and chile jam

I've included this recipe here because it is one thing that I love to have in my refrigerator at all times. It has a depth and pungency that I find irresistible and it goes with so many things—I especially adore it dolloped onto creamy scrambled eggs piled onto broiled sourdough toast for Sunday brunch. It also works brilliantly on top of broiled scallops, broiled lamb chops, or rare roast beef—alongside homemade horseradish cream, green beans, and little oily black olives.

for the jam

3 pounds Slow-Roasted Tomatoes (page 29)

1 tbsp yellow mustard seeds

2/3 cup red wine vinegar

3 ounces peeled fresh gingerroot, chopped

7 cloves garlic, peeled and chopped

5 fresh red chiles, chopped

3/4 cup superfine sugar (or scant 2/3 cup jaggery)

4 tbsp fish sauce

Put the roasted tomatoes into a large pan. Toast the mustard seeds in a skillet over low heat until they begin to pop. Remove and pound to a fine powder, using a mortar and pestle. Add to the tomatoes along with all the other ingredients.

Place over very low heat and cook gently for 2 hours, stirring regularly so that the mixture doesn't stick to the bottom. You will at the end have a delicious, inky-stained chutney.

Store in the refrigerator in a covered bowl for a week or so, or in sterilized jars in a cool place for up to 3 months.

Pickled pear relish

Anjou, Bosc, and Comice pears all work well in this delicious relish. It keeps well in the refrigerator for a week, so you might like to double or triple the quantities, giving you some to serve later on with cheese and cold meats. It is especially good with broiled sourdough bread and manchego, creamy dolcelatte, and cold roasted lamb. I also serve it with Cauliflower Soup with Gorgonzola and Pickled Pear Relish (page 150).

for the relish

2 tbsp dried cranberries

1 tbsp currants

2 firm, ripe pears

1 Golden Delicious apple

2 tbsp unsalted butter

5 tbsp cider or red wine vinegar

2 tbsp superfine sugar

3 thyme sprigs (ideally, lemon)

1 cinnamon stick

sea salt and freshly ground black pepper

Soak the dried cranberries and currants in a little bowl of warm water for 10 minutes or so—to soften them slightly. Core and chop the pears and apple into small dice (I like to leave the skin on).

Melt the butter in a small pan over low heat. When it begins to foam, add the diced fruit and cook for 5 minutes until starting to soften. Add all the other ingredients (except salt and pepper) and cook for another 8 to 10 minutes. The relish will have a shiny jewel-like luster. Taste and season, if necessary. Remove the cinnamon and thyme. Serve warm.

You can keep the relish in a covered bowl in the refrigerator for a week or so, or in a sterilized jar in the refrigerator for up to a month.

Flavored yogurts

I use flavored yogurts mostly in conjunction with dishes that have the toolbox spice mix as their foundation. Very often, these dishes are North African or Middle Eastern in feel and their earthy, pungent flavors are well softened by a top hat of yogurt. It rounds off the flavors, leaving them more palatable and gentle in the mouth. Thick, strained plain yogurt is the best kind to use for flavored yogurts. It has an unctuous quality and holds additional flavoring much more effectively than thin, light yogurt.

In the recipes where I have used specific flavored yogurts, I have listed all their ingredients. The following toolbox recipe is a basic flavor mix that works extremely well with many roasted meats, pickled vegetables, and slow-roasted tomatoes. You could replace the mint with cilantro, use a little chopped fresh red chile instead of Tabasco, or add some crushed garlic and/or grated fresh gingerroot if you like.

for the flavored yogurt

2 cups thick, strained plain yogurt
2 tsp Tabasco
grated zest and juice of 2 limes
20 mint leaves, minced
good pinch of sea salt
2 tbsp extra virgin olive oil

In a bowl, mix the yogurt with the Tabasco, lime zest and juice, mint, and salt, then incorporate the olive oil, beating well. Cover and refrigerate the yogurt until ready to use. It will taste pure only for a couple of days.

Season food with care and caution. Salt is probably the most critical of all ingredients in the kitchen. Used wisely, it enhances and turns up the volume on an ingredient's natural flavors. Use too little and you are not doing justice to a dish; use too much and the natural beauty of a dish is hidden behind an overpowering and abrasive taste. I always use sea salt.

Mayonnaise bases

Mayonnaise bases work in a similar way to flavored yogurts. They round out and complete dishes, adding a complexity to the final flavor. A variety of ingredients can be added to a mayonnaise to make it compatible to what you are cooking, including roasted ground almonds and other nuts, saffron, rosemary, garlic, lemon zest, anchovy, basil oil, even puréed roasted tomatoes. These mayonnaise bases work particularly well with the more Mediterranean flavors of tomato-based dishes. The purest mayonnaise base of all is simply enhanced with lemon juice and zest. This works beautifully with crab, white fish, shellfish, and any of the really glorious summer vegetables such as asparagus, fava beans, and peas.

I use only extra virgin olive oil when making mayonnaise, but if you find the flavor too intense, substitute half the quantity with sunflower-seed oil. Using a food processor is an easy method. The only trick is to pour the oil very slowly—too quickly and the mayonnaise may split.

This is the basic recipe. Of course, you can create many different flavored mayonnaises. Just remember to add the extra ingredients at the beginning with your egg yolks.

for the mayonnaise

3 organic egg yolks
juice of 1 lemon
2 tsp Dijon mustard
sea salt and freshly ground black pepper
generous 3/4 cup extra virgin olive oil

Place the egg yolks in a food processor and add the lemon juice, mustard, and a good pinch each of salt and pepper. Whiz briefly to combine. Pour the olive oil into a pitcher and then, with the motor running, pour it slowly through the feed tube in a fine stream until it is all incorporated and the mayonnaise is emulsified.

If the mayonnaise splits, it can usually be rectified by adding 1 tbsp warm water, then incorporating the rest of the oil. If this fails, pour the split mixture into a pitcher. Wash and dry the food processor, add another egg yolk, and with the motor running, drip the split mixture in, as if it were the oil, then incorporate the remaining oil.

For saffron mayonnaise, I infuse 15 to 20 saffron threads in 1 to 2 tbsp hot water for 10 minutes, then add the saffron and infused liquor right at the start.

To make aïoli, I simply add 3 finely puréed garlic cloves at the beginning, with the mustard and lemon juice.

Vinaigrettes

Because I serve so much food at room temperature, I often use vinaigrettes. Cooked and left to cool to a temperate degree is often the best way to appreciate the complex, natural flavors of many vegetables, fish, and meat. Indeed, my favorite way to start a meal is with a *salade composé*— a composition of different seasonal produce brought together with a simple vinaigrette.

I vary vinaigrettes according to the season and the food I am dressing. In summer, I tend to use a simple dressing—perhaps a spoonful of basil oil, a drizzle of olive oil, a squeeze of lemon juice, and a sprinkling of lemon zest. During the colder months, a dressing with a little more depth and heart is called for and I love to use different nut oils, gently warming them through first.

Where I have used specific vinaigrettes, I have listed the ingredients in the individual recipes. This is a simple, versatile vinaigrette and you can use a different vinegar and/or oil as you like, to alter its character.

for the basic vinaigrette

1 tbsp Dijon mustard
1 tbsp sherry vinegar
sea salt and freshly ground black pepper
generous 3/4 cup extra virgin olive oil
juice of 1/2 lemon

Put the mustard and vinegar into a bowl and add a generous pinch each of salt and pepper. Place the bowl on a cloth to keep it steady, then gradually whisk in the olive oil to emulsify. Lastly, squeeze in the lemon juice, and whisk to combine. Taste and adjust the seasoning and set aside until ready to use.

If the vinaigrette separates before you are ready to use it, give it a vigorous whisk and it will re-emulsify.

It is important to understand that when flavors are put together, they need a little time to become acquainted. This certainly applies to sauces, mayonnaises, and vinaigrettes. So, wait about 10 minutes before tasting and adjusting the seasoning. Once the ingredients have married, you may find that you need something quite different from what you first suspected, or indeed nothing at all.

Taste is about substance and wholeness ... without these components, a dish remains unmemorable. Each and every aspect of a recipe needs to be just right—no element should be ignored, otherwise its final outcome will feel careless.

Basil oil

This sludgy, verdant sauce lends a vibrancy to many of the dishes that I cook. Its flavor is clean and punchy and it works almost as a cleanser with many dishes, making the ingredients sing. It is definitely a pure, clean note toward the top end of the scale.

for the basil oil

3 large bunches of basil
1 clove garlic, peeled
sea salt and freshly ground black pepper
generous 3/4 cup extra virgin olive oil

Pull the basil leaves from their stalks and put them into a food processor with the garlic and a good pinch each of salt and pepper. Process until the basil is minced. With the motor running, slowly trickle in the olive oil through the feed tube and continue to blend until you have a beautiful moss green purée. Let stand for a few minutes, then taste and adjust the seasoning.

Pour into a jar, cover, and refrigerate until ready to use. This basil oil will keep well in the refrigerator for up to a week.

When I talk about bunches of herbs in a recipe, I mean just that—old-fashioned, generous bunches, as opposed to the mean-spirited little gathering of leaves to be found in plastic packages in grocery stores. Always think abundantly when you prepare food ... the finest cooking is about generosity of spirit!

Flavored oils

I'm not a fan of store-bought flavored oils—I've yet to come across any that I like. They oxidize so easily, losing any clarity of flavor in the process. I therefore make my own, using many different flavorings and the best olive oil I can afford. These oils are best used soon after they are prepared. Chile, garlic, and lemon-infused oils are the ones that I use most often.

Chile oil

I use this oil to give a dish a gentle kick, not an intense overwhelming heat. I therefore use the large fresh red chiles, which are fairly mild in flavor, and remove their seeds.

To prepare, halve 4 large fresh chiles lengthwise and remove the seeds. Slice lengthwise into very fine strips, then cut across into tiny squares (almost mincing the chiles). Place in a bowl, add a pinch of sea salt, and then pour over a generous 3/4 cup olive oil. Use the oil immediately or within 1 or 2 days.

Garlic oil

I am drawn to strong, clean flavors in food and I love the gutsy punch of chopped raw garlic. I am not afraid to throw raw garlic onto many dishes, especially if its rawness is slightly tempered by a good-quality olive oil. I often fold a spoonful or two of garlic oil into lemon mayonnaise or a flavored yogurt to give it a kick. And a bowl of cranberry or white beans comes alive if you stir in a spoonful or two just before eating.

To prepare, peel 10 garlic cloves, chop them very finely, and place in a bowl with a good pinch of sea salt. Pour over a generous 3/4 cup extra virgin olive oil and stir to combine. Use the oil immediately or within a day or two.

Lemon-infused oil

This is a fragrant, delicately flavored oil that is lovely spooned over broiled white fish; or used to dress a salad or hot vegetables, such as little potatoes, cauliflower, or broccoli; or drizzled onto sourdough toast with slow-roasted tomatoes and a young lemony goat cheese.

To prepare, use a swivel vegetable peeler to remove the zest from 2 unwaxed lemons in large strips. (This is the easiest way to take the zest thinly, leaving the bitter pith behind.) Warm a generous 3/4 cup extra virgin or good olive oil in a small pan over low heat. Add the finely pared lemon zest and leave over the lowest possible heat for 10 minutes to let the delicate citrusy flavor infuse the oil. Remove from the heat and let cool completely. Use the oil immediately or keep it in an airtight container for no longer than a day or two.

Lemon zest

The zesting of a lemon could never be described as a recipe, but this is an ingredient I use so often that it warrants a mention here in the toolbox. Its citrusy sharpness adds a dimension to so much of my food and I often use it as a garnish. For example, it partners with minced raw garlic and chopped parsley brilliantly to create gremolata, the classic *osso bucco* garnish that I use to finish many slow-cooked dishes.

Lemon zest works beautifully when tossed into a simple salad whose leaves include basil, mint, chervil, and arugula. The addition of grated Parmesan, lemon juice, and good olive oil is all that is needed, in my mind, to create a perfect green salad.

The tangy zest also cleans up the flavor of many desserts that would otherwise seem a fraction too sweet. Similarly, it works well to counteract the potentially cloying flavor of pickled fruits. In essence, lemon zest is a simple, quick way to add freshness to your cooking. There is no real secret, just be sure to use the finest holes on your grater and only use the yellow part of the skin. The white pith tends to taste very bitter. Grate your zest as close as possible to the time that you are going to use it, as it will dry out fairly quickly if left out uncovered, or indeed even covered in the refrigerator overnight.

Top note herbs

While base note herbs form the beginning of many dishes on which you layer other flavors, top note herbs are like the frosting on the cake—they complete the dish. My top note herbs are largely summer herbs—basil, parsley, cilantro, mint, chervil, and arugula—with their sharp clean flavors. These herbs don't tend to hold their flavor through vigorous cooking but must be added very close to the end of a dish, even if only as a garnish, to maintain their clarity and vibrancy.

A few herbs fall into both base and top note categories—parsley (Italian and curly) is one, while tarragon is another. Also, cilantro roots and stalks can lend base flavor to long-cooked dishes, whereas their leaves lose their character almost the moment they are exposed to high heat. I would rarely use woody, earthy base note herbs to finish a dish. To my mind, a garnish should always be light and sing the high notes with its flavors.

THE SEASONS

Spring

I am always thrilled to welcome spring because it brings such an abundance of beautiful produce—rhubarb, apricots, new carrots, beets, fennel, chards, morels, fava beans, radishes, sweet herbs, and soft, lemony goat cheeses. It is also the season for early asparagus, sweet peas, young leeks, lobsters, scallops, late oysters, and, of course, exquisite spring lamb.

With the exception of early October, there is no more beautiful time to celebrate the seasons. As the days begin earlier, the land begins to wake up from its long winter sleep. Bulbs flower almost overnight and life appears a little brighter and happier.

Salad of spring vegetables with herbs, romano, and lemon-infused oil

This is a celebration of the wonderful sweet vegetables that become available during late spring. I grew up in Australia and I love the heat, but there is something so particular and gentle about a warm late spring day in the UK. Somehow this salad epitomizes everything that is lovely here at this time of the year. If you can't find a young romano cheese, use feta instead.

Serves 4

1 bunch of asparagus (about 10 spears)

1¹/2 cups freshly podded fava beans

1 cup freshly podded young English peas

sea salt and freshly ground black pepper

4 tbsp Lemon-Infused Oil (toolbox, page 44)

small handful of basil leaves

small handful of mint leaves

handful of arugula leaves

6 ounces young romano, thinly sliced

¹/4 cup Roasted Red Onions (toolbox, page 29), optional

grated lemon zest, to taste

lemon juice, to taste

finely pared lemon zest, to garnish (optional)

Place a large pot of well-salted water on to boil. Snap the woody ends off the asparagus. Using a swivel vegetable peeler, finely peel the skin from the bottom third of the stalks. When the water is boiling rapidly, drop in the asparagus and allow to return to a boil, then cook for 45 seconds, or until just tender. Remove the asparagus spears from the pan with tongs and put into a colander. Refresh under cold running water.

Add the fava beans to the pot, allow the water to come back to a boil, and cook for 45 seconds. Remove with a slotted spoon and tip into a colander, then refresh under cold running water. When cool, slip off the dull greenish gray skins to reveal the delicate green beans hidden inside.

To cook the peas, drop them into the same boiling water, return to a boil, and cook for 1 minute. Drain and refresh in the same way.

To assemble, gently pat the asparagus, peas, and fava beans dry and place in a bowl. Season with salt and pepper and spoon over a little of the lemon-infused oil. Set aside.

Combine the herb and arugula leaves in another bowl. Spoon over a little of the lemony oil, season, and toss lightly with your fingers.

To serve, pile the leaves onto a large plate or divide among serving plates. Arrange the romano slices, fava beans, peas, and asparagus on top, adding the roasted red onion slices too, if using. Drizzle over the rest of the oil and scatter over a few herb leaves. A sprinkling of lemon zest and a squeeze or two of lemon juice would not go amiss.

Morels on toast

Looking almost as though they are mushrooms that belong to another world, morels are wonderful to eat. They are usually around during late February and early March, depending on the weather, though often fearfully expensive. To make the cost a little more bearable, I have paired them here with portobello mushrooms. If you're feeling really extravagant, use all morels! On the other hand, if you're feeling poor, portobellos taste pretty good on their own, treated in this simple way.

Serves 4

1 pound 2 ounces morels

1 pound 2 ounces portobello mushrooms

4 slices of chewy peasant-style bread

1 clove garlic, halved

1 tbsp extra virgin olive oil, to drizzle

2 tbsp unsalted butter

sea salt and freshly ground black pepper

juice of 1/2 lemon

1 tbsp Dijon mustard

generous 3/4 cup crème fraîche

1 tbsp minced curly parsley

Start by cleaning the morels. I use a mushroom brush (though a pastry brush is fine if you haven't got one). Gentle brushing (rather than washing) helps to remove the dirt but not the flavor. Check the morels carefully for bugs. Wipe the portobello mushrooms clean with a damp cloth and break them in half with your fingers.

Toast the bread under a broiler on both sides. Rub all over with the cut garlic clove and drizzle with the olive oil.

Melt the butter in a large skillet over a medium heat. When it is sizzling, add the portobello mushrooms and cook for about 2 minutes. Season generously with salt and pepper.

Add the morels and cook for a minute or so, without stirring. Squeeze over the lemon juice and leave the mushrooms alone once again to cook for another 2 minutes. This results in a lovely, meaty texture (if you stir them continuously, they will stew).

Add the mustard and crème fraîche, stir to combine, then increase the heat to allow the cream to bubble and thicken slightly.

Now, taste and adjust the seasoning—you will probably need a little more salt and pepper. Spoon the mushrooms on top of the toast and sprinkle with the parsley. Serve straight away!

I season twice during cooking—once in the early stages to tickle and encourage flavors to show themselves, then finally just before serving to pull everything together. I don't season in between because all dishes change in flavor as they are cooking. I like to let them find their own feet in the time in between.

Warm asparagus with herb mayonnaise

Asparagus has a short glorious season in the UK, straddling late spring and early summer—just six weeks from around the beginning of May. In the United States, the traditional season runs from March into mid-June. I choose to eat it only during its short stay, never feeling tempted to buy asparagus grown in foreign climates. There are many ways to enjoy it while it is here. Peeling the stalks might seem an old-fashioned way of presenting asparagus, but I find the pale, greeny white flesh underneath beautiful, especially against the vibrant green of the just-cooked asparagus tips.

Serves 4
2 bunches of asparagus
(20 to 24 spears)
sea salt and freshly ground
black pepper

Herb mayonnaise
2/3 cup Mayonnaise (toolbox,
page 36)
1 tbsp chopped chives
1 tbsp chopped tarragon
leaves
1 tbsp minced curly parsley
1 tbsp chopped basil
1/4 cup crème fraîche

To serve
extra virgin olive oil (ideally,
a mild kind, such as Ligurian)
lemon wedges

First, prepare the mayonnaise. Stir the chopped herbs and crème fraîche into the basic mayonnaise and adjust the seasoning if necessary. Set aside.

While you prepare the asparagus, put a pot of well-salted water on to boil. Snap the asparagus stalks close to the base to remove their woody ends. Using a swivel vegetable peeler, finely peel the skin from the bottom third of the stalks.

When the water is boiling steadily, drop in the asparagus. Bring back to a boil and cook until just tender—this takes very little time, usually no more than 45 seconds.

Drain the asparagus immediately and place on warm serving plates. Drizzle with a few drops of olive oil and serve with the herb mayonnaise and a wedge of lemon on the side.

All green vegetables should be cooked in well-salted water—salty as seawater. This helps to keep their color vibrant and their taste pure.

Fava beans with mint, ricotta, and crisp prosciutto

The feeling of this dish is very light and clean. Crispy, paper-thin sheets of prosciutto lend a lovely, slightly salty-sweet contrast to the spring flavors of fava beans, mint, and fresh, sweet ricotta. It is ideal for a light lunch, which I would finish with a bowl of fresh apricots and ginger tea.

Serves 4

3 cups freshly podded fava beans (about 2¹/4 pounds in the pod)

sea salt and freshly ground black pepper

small bunch of mint, stems removed

5 tbsp extra virgin olive oil, plus extra to drizzle

8 slices of prosciutto

4 slices of good-quality bread, (*pane toscana* or ciabatta)

1 clove garlic, halved

1 cup fresh ricotta

2 ounces Parmesan, freshly grated

finely grated zest and juice of 1 lemon, or to taste

Preheat the oven to 375°F (convection oven to 350°F). Place a pot of well-salted water on to boil. When it is boiling steadily, add the fava beans and wait for the water to return to a boil. Cook for another 20 seconds only. Drain the fava beans and quickly refresh in cold water. Drain well, then peel off the pale greenish gray outer layer, to reveal the tender green beans. Set aside.

Mince the mint leaves, saving a few whole leaves for garnish. Put the chopped mint into a bowl with the 5 tbsp olive oil, stir well, and set aside to infuse for 10 minutes.

Season the fava beans with salt and pepper, drizzle with a little of the mint-infused oil, and toss to mix.

Lay the prosciutto slices side by side on a baking sheet and drizzle with a little olive oil and pepper. Place in the hot oven and roast

until crisp, 8 to 10 minutes. In the meantime, toast or broil the bread until golden brown. Rub with the cut garlic clove and drizzle with a little olive oil.

Put the ricotta into a bowl and fold in the Parmesan, two-thirds of the lemon zest, half of the lemon juice, and a drizzle of the minty oil. Season with salt and pepper. Taste and adjust the flavor if necessary—it should be clean, creamy, fresh, and vibrant.

Lay the toast slices on individual plates. Spoon the ricotta mixture onto the toast, then pile the fava beans on top. Arrange the crisp, warm, prosciutto on the salad and scatter over a few of the reserved mint leaves. Spoon on a little more mint-infused oil, sprinkle with the rest of the lemon zest, and squeeze over the last of the lemon juice to serve.

Leeks vinaigrette with eggs mimosa, capers, and black olives

A timeless classic, leeks vinaigrette makes a lovely appetizer. I've added eggs mimosa (so-called because they resemble the flower), and capers and olives for sharpness and depth. Sourdough bread crumbs can also add a delightful textural contrast, or you might prefer to serve some good, crusty, open-textured white bread on the side. Choose small, firm leeks with a good proportion of white flesh. Dress while still warm, as this encourages them to soak up the flavor of the vinaigrette.

Serves 4

20 to 24 trimmed young leeks, well washed

generous 3/4 cup verjuice (see page 81)

1¼ cups water

8 whole black peppercorns

4 thyme sprigs

3 bay leaves

Vinaigrette

1½ tsp Dijon mustard

1 tbsp light cream

sea salt and freshly ground black pepper

1½ tbsp red wine vinegar

scant ⅓ cup extra virgin olive oil

To finish

2 organic eggs, hard-cooked

1 tbsp capers preserved in salt, well rinsed in tepid water

handful of black olives (ideally, Niçoise or Ligurian)

small bunch of curly parsley, stalks removed and minced

Check that the leeks are thoroughly clean (they can hold dirt all the way down to the stem). Pour the verjuice and water into a pan (large enough to hold all the leeks) and add the peppercorns, thyme, and bay leaves. Place over medium heat and bring to a gentle boil, then add the leeks. Turn down the heat slightly and simmer gently for 8 to 10 minutes, or until tender. Meanwhile, make the dressing.

For the vinaigrette, put the mustard and cream into a small bowl, add a little salt and pepper, and whisk together. Add the vinegar and stir to combine. Now, slowly add the olive oil in a thin steady stream, whisking constantly to emulsify. Set aside for 5 minutes or so, to allow the flavors to get to know each other.

Meanwhile, peel the hard-cooked eggs and grate on the finest holes of your grater—they should have a very light texture.

As soon as the leeks are cooked, remove them from the pan and drain on paper towels. Lay them neatly on top of each other on warm plates and spoon over half of the vinaigrette. Scatter the grated eggs, capers, and olives randomly on top. Drizzle over the last of the vinaigrette, dust with pepper, and sprinkle with minced parsley to serve.

Spinach soup with nutmeg and crème fraîche

Every time I make this soup, I am excited and dazzled by its beautiful, mossy green color. Sludgy in texture, it has a fresh, light taste. The trick is to hardly cook the spinach at all, in order to keep its strong, clear color.

Serves 4

10 ounces young, tender spinach leaves

2 tbsp unsalted butter

2 large shallots, peeled and finely sliced

1 clove garlic, peeled and minced

sea salt and freshly ground black pepper

4 cups Chicken Stock (toolbox, page 18)

generous 1/3 cup crème fraîche

1/2 tsp freshly grated nutmeg, or to taste

grated lemon zest, to sprinkle (optional)

Start by washing the spinach really well in several changes of water. Spinach tends to hold dirt, so make sure you wash it until the water runs clear. Drain and shake the spinach dry.

Place a large pan (big enough to hold the spinach) over medium-high heat. Add the spinach and cook until it just wilts (the water clinging to the leaves after washing generates enough steam for cooking). Drain in a colander and set aside.

Rinse and dry the pan. Add the butter and melt gently over low heat until softly foaming, then add the shallots and sweat for 5 minutes, or until softened and translucent. Add the garlic and cook for a minute or two, then season generously with salt and pepper.

Add the spinach and stir once or twice to combine, then pour in the stock and turn up the heat. Bring to a simmer, then immediately remove from the heat. Purée the soup in a blender, in batches as necessary, until velvety smooth.

Return the soup to the pan and stir in the crème fraîche. Add the grated nutmeg, then check for seasoning—adding a little more nutmeg, pepper, and/or salt to taste. Reheat gently ... there's nothing worse than soup that's not hot enough. I like to add a sprinkling of grated lemon zest before serving.

Celery and leek soup with truffle oil

I am always amazed that so many people say they don't like celery. The inner white heart is one of the finest things I could eat, especially on a warm day, when its delicious watery crunch is so refreshing. The importance of celery in cooking shouldn't be underestimated either, as it has a fundamental role in the making of a good stock and lends character to many slow-cooked dishes.

Serves 4

1 small head of celery, about 14 ounces trimmed

2 leeks (white part only)

4 tbsp unsalted butter

2 medium or 1 large potato, peeled and chopped

2 bay leaves

2 or 3 thyme sprigs

1 or 2 Italian parsley stems

sea salt and freshly ground black pepper

4 cups Chicken Stock (toolbox, page 18)

2/3 cup heavy cream

truffle oil, to drizzle

Separate the celery stalks and peel them finely, then chop roughly. Wash and chop the leeks. Melt the butter in a large pan over low heat. Add the celery and leeks and cook gently for 15 minutes or so, until the celery is soft but not colored.

Add the potato, bay leaves, thyme, and parsley and season with a pinch or two of salt and a little pepper. Pour in the stock and bring to a boil, then lower the heat and simmer gently for 20 minutes.

Remove from the heat and discard the herbs. Purée the soup in small batches in a blender, very thoroughly. Pass through a chinois (not a fine-meshed one) back into the pan to ensure a smooth, creamy texture.

Pour in the cream and reheat gently. Check the seasoning and serve topped with a restrained drizzle of truffle oil.

Another old-fashioned idea of mine is that celery eaten raw should be peeled. It's an attention to detail—like mincing parsley very finely or peeling the ends of asparagus—that makes all the difference to a well-considered dish.

Baked ricotta with roasted tomatoes, black olives, and basil oil

This is a delicious way to serve ricotta and you can cook it a day ahead if it makes life simpler. The flavor is more interesting if you allow it to cool to room temperature—it will also be easier to slice. You can use the baked ricotta slices as a base for a more elaborate antipasti plate—adding salami, bresaola, marinated artichokes, and/or broiled pepper, if you like.

Serves 6

olive oil, to brush pan

1 pound 2 ounces ricotta cheese

2 organic eggs, beaten

8 ounces Parmesan, freshly grated

grated zest of 1 lemon

1 tbsp soft thyme leaves, minced

sea salt and freshly ground black pepper

To serve

about 12 Slow-Roasted Tomato halves (toolbox, page 29)

handful of black olives (ideally, Niçoise or Ligurian)

1/3 cup Basil Oil (toolbox, page 42)

handful of arugula leaves, tossed in a little lemon juice and olive oil (optional)

Preheat the oven to 325°F (convection oven to 300°F). Brush a nonstick 8 1/2 by 4 1/2-inch loaf pan with a little olive oil.

In a large bowl, whisk together the ricotta and eggs until smooth. Add the Parmesan, lemon zest, and thyme. Stir lightly to combine and season with salt and pepper to taste.

Spoon the mixture into the prepared pan, place in a roasting pan, and pour in enough water to come halfway up the sides of the loaf pan. Carefully place in the oven and bake until the ricotta is firm, 30 to 40 minutes. Set aside to cool to room temperature.

When cooled, carefully turn out onto a cutting board and cut into slices with a sharp knife. Arrange the slices on individual plates and add a couple of roasted tomatoes, a few black olives, and a spoonful of basil oil. Also, a tangle of dressed arugula does not go amiss.

Mezze plate

This plate of different flavors was inspired by a delicious lunch I had in a Moroccan restaurant in Sydney, called Cafe Mint—I strongly recommend a visit if you should ever be passing that way. These dips work beautifully together, or you can serve any of them separately, with other "bits and pieces" as you like. All of the dips keep well in the refrigerator for up to 5 days.

Roasted tomato and red pepper purée

This delicious purée has a wonderful rustic quality. It sits happily on the mezze plate, but would also be lovely served with broiled firm-fleshed white fish or chicken.

Serves 4

4 red bell peppers

2 red onions, peeled and roughly chopped

4 cloves garlic, peeled and roughly chopped

6 plum tomatoes, roughly chopped

2 fresh red chiles, sliced

bunch of cilantro

1 tbsp Roasted Spice Mix (toolbox, page 16)

1 tbsp dried mint

1 tbsp extra virgin olive oil

1 tbsp good-quality balsamic vinegar

sea salt and freshly ground black pepper

1/2 cup plain yogurt

1/2 bunch of mint, leaves only

Preheat the oven to 250°F (convection oven to 225°F). Halve, core, and seed the bell peppers, making sure you remove all the white pith and membrane. Put the peppers into a roasting pan with the onions, garlic, tomatoes, and chiles.

Separate the cilantro leaves and set aside; mince the stems and scatter over the vegetables. Sprinkle with the spice mix and dried mint, then drizzle over the olive oil and vinegar. Season with salt and pepper and toss to mix. Slow-roast in the oven, stirring occasionally, until the red peppers are soft and slightly caramelized, 30 to 40 minutes.

Remove from the oven and let cool to room temperature, then whiz in a blender with the yogurt, mint, and reserved cilantro leaves until smooth. Taste the purée and adjust the seasoning—it will almost certainly need more salt.

Balsamic vinegar is a particularly special ingredient. I don't mean the cheap imposter found in most grocery stores, but true balsamic vinegar made from a saba base and aged for at least 12 years. This fine product is soft and sweet, viscous in texture, with no hint of acidity. It may be very expensive, but it is worth every cent—3 or 4 drops is all that you need to take a dish to a different level.

Beet purée

This striking purée is a staple item on our mezze plate. Its zingy, spiciness allows it to stand proudly on its own, too, so it's worth making extra. I love it simply spread on toast, and with griddled scallops.

Serves 6

3 pounds beets
sea salt
2 cloves garlic, peeled
1 large fresh red chile
bunch of cilantro
1/2 bunch of mint, leaves only
1 tbsp grated fresh horseradish
1 tbsp Roasted Spice Mix (toolbox, page 16)
3 tbsp good-quality balsamic vinegar, or to taste
2 tbsp olive oil
1/2 cup thick, strained plain yogurt

Put the beets in a pan, add cold water to cover, and season with a little salt. Bring to a boil over high heat, then turn down the heat and simmer until the beets are tender when pierced with a fork—this may take a good 40 minutes. Drain and let the beets cool slightly, then remove the skins and stalks.

Place the cooked beets in a blender with the garlic and chile. Chop the cilantro stems and add to the blender with the cilantro and mint leaves, horseradish, spice mix, vinegar, and olive oil. Blend well to a smooth purée.

Add the yogurt and pulse quickly, just once or twice. Taste for seasoning—the purée will definitely need salt to bring all the flavors together. You may also need a few more drops of vinegar—it needs a sharp edge.

Chickpea purée

This purée is only really good if all the flavors are strong and clear. It should taste vibrant, not merely like a hummus, so be prepared to adjust the flavors as necessary. Although I most often serve it as part of the mezze, this chickpea purée also works really well with broiled or roast lamb.

Serves 4

11/2 cups cooked chickpeas
2 cloves garlic, peeled
1 large fresh red chile
bunch of cilantro
bunch of mint, leaves only
juice of 1 lemon, or to taste
1 tbsp sesame seed paste
2 tbsp strained plain yogurt
11/2 tsp Roasted Spice Mix (toolbox, page 16)
3 tbsp extra virgin olive oil
sea salt and freshly ground black pepper

Drain the chickpeas (rinse as well if using canned ones). Place the cooked chickpeas in a blender or food processor with the garlic and chile. Chop the cilantro stems and add to the blender with the cilantro and mint leaves. Add the rest of the ingredients, including a little salt and pepper, and blend to a purée (don't overprocess).

Taste and adjust the seasoning, perhaps adding more lemon and a little more salt than you might expect. Salt definitely helps to bring all the flavors together here.

Mezze salad

A simple mixed leaf and herb salad complements the purées perfectly. Of course, you can vary the salad greens as you like. The light, lemony dressing is subtle, so as not to detract from the other flavors in the mezze.

Serves 4

handful of dandelion leaves

handful of arugula leaves

handful of ruby chard or other young, tender red chard

10 mint leaves

10 basil leaves

small bunch of chervil, leaves only

sea salt and freshly ground black pepper

finely grated zest of 1 lemon

1/4 cup extra virgin olive oil

juice of 1/2 lemon

Wash and pat dry the salad and herb leaves and place in a bowl. Season with a generous pinch of salt and a little pepper, then sprinkle with the lemon zest. Drizzle with the olive oil and squeeze over the lemon juice. Toss together lightly with your fingers to serve.

Mezze plate

As I arrange the different elements of the mezze on the plate, I like to add a few roasted tomatoes, a little fresh goat cheese, and a scattering of braised lentils, but you could leave the lentils out to keep it simpler if you prefer. A drizzle of basil oil brings it all together on the plate.

Roasted Tomato and Red Pepper Purée (page 67)

Beet Purée (left)

Chickpea Purée (left)

Mezze Salad (above)

8 Slow-Roasted Tomato halves (toolbox, page 29)

4 tbsp soft, fresh lemony goat cheese or ricotta (optional)

1/2 cup Braised Lentils (toolbox, page 22), optional

Basil Oil (toolbox, page 42), to drizzle

To assemble your mezze, place a large spoonful of each purée on each individual serving plate and pile the dressed salad alongside. Put a couple of roasted tomato halves and a little goat cheese on top and scatter some braised lentils around. Drizzle with basil oil and serve.

Crab salad with nam jim and mixed cress

Really good fresh crabmeat is a rich and pure delicacy that needs to be served as simply as possible and the clean, clear Asian flavors of nam jim work perfectly. This simple, hot Thai dressing also goes well with barbecued seafood and cold sliced rare beef tenderloin. It is best prepared shortly before using, as the flavors intensify the longer they sit. I have taken the liberty of adjusting the chiles for a gentler taste—the traditional recipe calls for at least five times the amount!

Serves 4

1 pound 2 ounces freshly prepared crabmeat (ordered from your fish supplier)

handful of mixed cress or wild arugula leaves

1 large, mild fresh red chile, finely sliced (optional)

Nam jim

2 cloves garlic, peeled

bunch of cilantro, stems only

sea salt

1 fresh green Thai chile, chopped

2 tbsp jaggery or superfine sugar

2 tbsp fish sauce

3 tbsp lime juice, or to taste

2 red shallots, peeled and minced

To serve

lime wedges

First, make the nam jim (as close to serving as possible). Using a mortar and pestle, pound the garlic and cilantro stems with a pinch of salt until well crushed. Add the green chile and continue to pound. Mix in the sugar, fish sauce, and lime juice, then stir in the shallots. Before serving, taste and adjust the flavors as necessary, perhaps adding a little more salt or lime juice.

Dress the crab with about 4 tbsp nam jim—enough to give it a clean, clear, sweet, hot flavor, but not too much; otherwise, it will overpower the delicate taste of the crab. Scatter the mixed cress through, along with the red chile for an extra kick. Serve with lime wedges on the side.

Mixed cress is something I get periodically from Andrew, my vegetable supplier. It includes pea cress, radish cress, shiso (Japanese cress), and garlic shoots. These make a deliciously tangly knot that is visually very beautiful. Mixed cress isn't easy to find, but you could try asking your grocery store if they could get hold of one or two (if not all) of the varieties. Otherwise, peppery wild arugula is a satisfactory alternative.

Wild garlic is one of those special ingredients—
a seasonal treasure that I wait for with eager anticipation.
When cooked, these beautiful, dark green, delicate
leaves have the gentlest, smoothest essence of garlic
about them, which marries well with many of spring's
abundant ingredients. Ask your grocery store to order
them in for you, or better still hunt for them yourself.
They are most commonly found alongside bluebells in
woods. Freshly picked and quickly pan-fried in sweet,
unsalted butter, wild garlic leaves make a wonderful
accompaniment to spring lamb, roasted wild salmon, or
pan-fried morels and they are delicious with scrambled
eggs on toast. You can also eat them uncooked in a
simple salad with other leaves, but be warned—the raw
leaves have a much stronger, peppery, garlic taste.

I like fish to be cooked through, not translucent at the bone, and my cooking times reflect this. I serve fillets skin uppermost, so this needs to be crunchy, golden brown, and generously seasoned with salt. The flesh underneath must be succulent and just cooked through. Pan-frying fillets, skin side down, without moving until crisp, and finishing them off in the oven is the best way.

Pan-fried salmon with wild garlic

Please don't be tempted to use farmed salmon. Wild salmon has a far superior flavor, even compared with organic farmed salmon. Expensive it may be, but if you only eat wild salmon once this season, the memory of it will sustain you until you can afford it again! Here it is served with mellow wild garlic and a fragrant, herby green mayonnaise. If you cannot obtain wild garlic, this dish works well with young, tender spinach.

Serves 4

4 wild salmon fillets, about 6 ounces each

sea salt and freshly ground black pepper

2 tbsp olive oil

4 handfuls of wild garlic leaves, gently washed and patted dry

3 tbsp unsalted butter

Sauce verte

1 recipe Mayonnaise (toolbox, page 36)

small bunch of chervil

small bunch of tarragon, leaves only

small bunch of chives

2 tbsp crème fraîche

To serve

1 lemon, cut into 4 wedges

First, make the sauce verte. Have the mayonnaise ready. Mince the herbs together. Add them to the mayonnaise along with the crème fraîche and stir to combine. Taste and add a little more salt and pepper if needed. You should have a sauce that is light and fresh, both in taste and in consistency. Set aside until ready to use.

Preheat the oven to 425°F (convection oven to 400°F). Season the fish generously on the skin side and a little less so on the flesh side. Heat one large (or two smaller) nonstick ovenproof skillets over medium heat, then add the olive oil. When the skillet is really hot (you will see a faint haze begin to rise from the surface), add the salmon, skin side down.

Cook for 3 minutes, without turning, until the skin begins to crisp up and you see the flesh lose its translucency close to where it meets the skin. At this point, transfer the skillet(s) to the hot oven and allow the fish to cook for another 1 to 2 minutes, until just cooked. (However, overcooking salmon quickly dries the flesh and spoils the texture, so time carefully.)

Remove and set aside to rest in a warm place while you quickly cook the wild garlic. Melt the butter in a shallow pan over medium heat. When it just starts to foam, add the garlic and season with a little salt and a generous grinding of pepper. Cook for no longer than a minute, stirring to ensure the leaves are evenly wilted, then remove from the skillet.

To serve, place the salmon fillets, skin side up, on warm plates and pile the garlic alongside. Spoon over the sauce verte (or hand it around separately if you prefer) and serve with lemon wedges.

Mackerel fillets with roasted tomatoes and horseradish cream

Horseradish works well alongside oily fish. You really need to grate it freshly, though this may bring tears to your eyes! Mackerel needs to be exceptionally fresh to be delicious. Ask your fish supplier to fillet the fish for you—if the fillets are quite large, allow two per person; if small, then you will need to allow three. Mackerel also tastes best when it is very hot, so don't let it sit around before serving.

Serves 4

4 to 6 mackerel, filleted
sea salt and freshly ground black pepper
1 tbsp olive oil
12 to 16 Slow-Roasted Tomato halves (toolbox, page 29)

Horseradish cream

generous 3/4 cup crème fraîche
1 tbsp freshly grated horseradish
1¹/2 tsp Dijon mustard
sea salt and freshly ground black pepper

To serve

Roasted Red Onion slices (toolbox, page 29), optional
1 tbsp minced curly parsley
extra virgin olive oil, to drizzle

First, make the horseradish cream. Put the crème fraîche in a bowl and stir in the horseradish and mustard. Season with a pinch of salt and a tiny amount of pepper. (If making ahead, cover and refrigerate, but bring back to room temperature before serving.)

Preheat the oven to 425°F (convection oven to 400°F). Season the mackerel on both sides, but a little more generously on the skin side. Heat one large (or 2 smaller) nonstick ovenproof skillet over medium heat, then add the olive oil. When the skillet is hot and lightly smoking, add the mackerel fillets, skin side down, and cook without turning or moving until the skin is golden and crunchy. Put the skillet into the hot oven and cook for just under a minute, then remove.

To serve, layer the roasted tomato halves and mackerel fillets on warm serving plates, placing a dollop of horseradish cream on the bottom and top fillets. Finish with a tomato half and a few roasted onion slices. Sprinkle over the minced parsley, drizzle a little olive oil around the plate, and serve immediately.

A nonstick pan is invaluable in any kitchen—especially for pan-frying fish and meat, and for perfect fried eggs. Nonstick pans need to be well looked after. Don't use an abrasive scourer to clean them. I wrap mine in a dry dish towel to protect them while they are stored.

Lobster curry with tamarind, roasted coconut, ginger, and coriander

This dish is based upon a style of cooking that is typical along India's southwest coast, though I have added fish sauce and sugar, which are not traditional ingredients. If lobster seems too extravagant, you could use any clean, firm-fleshed fish—monkfish would be perfect.

Serves 4

sea salt and freshly ground black pepper

4 very fresh, live lobsters, about 1 pound 2 ounces each

3 tbsp vegetable oil

2 onions, peeled and finely sliced

2-inch piece fresh gingerroot, peeled and finely diced

4 cloves garlic, peeled and minced

2 fresh red chiles, chopped

1 tbsp coriander seeds, toasted

5 ripe tomatoes, chopped

1 tbsp superfine sugar

3 tbsp fish sauce

3 tbsp tamarind water (see page 205)

generous 2 1/2 cups canned coconut milk

1/2 cup unsweetened dried coconut flakes, lightly toasted

Bring a large pan of well-salted water to a fast boil, then drop in the lobsters and cook for 8 minutes. Remove from the pan and leave until cool enough to handle, then extract the meat. Take a sharp knife and make an incision all the way down the middle of the body. Remove the flesh and cut into medallions, discarding the stomach sac and the dark intestinal thread, which runs the length of the body. Crack the large claws with the back of a heavy knife and gently remove the meat. Save the legs for garnish.

Heat the oil in a heavy pan over medium heat. Add the onions, lower the heat a little, and cook gently, stirring every now and then, until they are translucent.

Meanwhile, put the ginger, garlic, chiles, coriander seeds, and tomatoes in a blender and whiz to a paste. Scrape out the mixture and add it to the onions in the pan. Cook, stirring frequently, for 5 minutes.

Add the sugar, fish sauce, and tamarind water and stir well, then pour in the coconut milk. Turn the heat to medium and simmer for 10 minutes. Add the cooked lobster and heat gently for 2 to 3 minutes, until it is just warmed through. Taste and adjust the seasoning.

Ladle the curry into warm bowls or soup plates and garnish with the reserved lobster legs and toasted coconut flakes to serve.

Buy live lobsters from your fish supplier—they will taste all the better for being so fresh. Order them in advance and check that they are still feisty when you collect them. Wrap in damp newspaper, keep in a box, and cook soon after buying. The kindest thing to do is pop the lobsters in the freezer for an hour or so before cooking—to put them into a deep sleep. Then, bring a large pot of well-salted water (as salty as the sea) to a boil. Drop in the sleepy lobsters and cook for 8 minutes exactly.

Rabbit, pancetta, and verjuice

I have cooked a lot of rabbit over the past year. I really enjoy its flavor and it proves to be very popular on the restaurant menu. I prefer the taste and texture of farmed, free-range rabbit to that of wild rabbit, which tends to be stronger in flavor, tougher, and sometimes riddled with shot. Longer, slower cooking works better for me with rabbit—I like it when the meat is so soft that it falls from the bone. If you prefer firmer flesh, simply reduce the cooking time by half.

Serves 4

3 pounds farmed free-range rabbit, jointed (or ask your butcher for 4 back legs)

sea salt and freshly ground black pepper

2 tbsp olive oil

6 slices of pancetta or bacon

1 large yellow onion, peeled and finely sliced

1/2 cup verjuice (or dry white wine)

2 tbsp Dijon mustard

3 bay leaves

2 thyme sprigs

3 cloves garlic, peeled and minced

1 1/4 cups Chicken Stock (toolbox, page 18)

2 tbsp crème fraîche

1 tbsp minced parsley

Preheat the oven to 325°F (convection oven to 300°F). Season the rabbit generously with salt and pepper. Place a Dutch oven or other heavy ovenproof pot (large enough to accommodate all the ingredients) over medium heat and add the olive oil. When it is hot and just smoking, add the rabbit pieces and brown them well all over. As they brown, remove the pieces and set aside.

Add the pancetta and onion to the pot, turn down the heat, and cook for 5 minutes, or until the pancetta is browned and the onion has started to soften.

Return the rabbit pieces to the pot, pour over the verjuice, and add the mustard. Turn up the heat a little, so the liquor bubbles, then add the bay leaves, thyme, and garlic, and pour on the stock. Put the lid on, place in the oven, and cook until the rabbit is very, very tender, 70 to 80 minutes.

Carefully remove the rabbit pieces and set aside. Place the pot over high heat and let the liquor bubble to reduce slightly. You want to thicken it a little and intensify the flavor. This should take no longer than 5 minutes.

Add the crème fraîche and stir to combine with the juices. Return the rabbit pieces to the pot and warm through for a minute or so. Check the seasoning and serve sprinkled with the minced parsley.

Verjuice is a sour juice extracted from unripe grapes. It lends a special flavor and is available from selected grocery stores and specialty food stores, but if you are unable to find it, use a dry white wine instead.

Chargriddled salt-crusted tenderloin of beef

I love to eat simply griddled beef tenderloin with a purée of potatoes and a peppery arugula salad. Crème fraîche spiked with freshly grated horseradish and hot English mustard is also a delicious condiment to serve on the side. Ask your butcher for a really good piece of tenderloin—look for an intense, deep red color and an even marbling of fat through the meat.

Serves 4

1 cup sea salt, about 7 ounces

2 tbsp freshly ground black pepper

vegetable oil, for oiling

2¹/4 pounds prime beef tenderloin

2 tbsp extra virgin olive oil

juice of 1 lemon

To serve

Horseradish Cream (page 134)

Sprinkle the salt and pepper on a small baking sheet to make a fairly even layer, about ¹/4 inch thick. Set the sheet aside, close to the stove.

Preheat a griddle or heavy nonstick pan and oil very lightly. Cut the beef tenderloin into 4 thick slices and place them on the hot griddle. Cook, without moving for 4 minutes, then turn and cook on the other side, undisturbed, for a further 4 minutes.

Carefully remove the meat and place on the salt-encrusted sheet. Turn the meat once so the seasoning coats both sides, then let rest for 15 minutes. (This resting stage is very important—don't skimp on it.)

Return the salt-encrusted steaks to the griddle and cook for another 1 minute on each side for rare to medium meat. Lift the meat back onto the baking sheet and let sit for another 2 to 3 minutes.

Transfer the beef to a cutting board, drizzle with the olive oil, and squeeze over the lemon juice. Cut into generous slices and arrange on warm plates. Serve with the horseradish cream and accompaniments.

All cooking, for me, relies heavily on the use of beautiful quality ingredients, treated with the utmost respect—sourced from people who care about what they raise and grow. I strongly recommend that you seek out good suppliers if possible. In particular, try to source meat from a local butcher with an excellent reputation.

Lamb chops with skordalia and spinach

Little lamb rib chops are delicious griddled or barbecued and served with skordalia—a Greek-style mashed potato, only much more. A good skordalia is garlicky, sharp, and tangy, with a texture that is slightly crunchy and creamy all at the same time. It tastes best at room temperature. Ask your butcher for French-trimmed chops.

Serves 4

12 lamb rib chops

sea salt and freshly ground black pepper

vegetable oil, if needed

Skordalia

5 cloves garlic (unpeeled)

2/3 cup blanched almonds

3 small-medium round waxy potatoes, such as Yukon Gold or Yellow Finn

finely grated zest and juice of 1 lemon

sea salt and freshly ground black pepper

scant 1/3 cup extra virgin olive oil

To serve

Spinach with Garlic, Lemon, and Chile (page 139)

First, make the skordalia. Preheat the oven to 325°F (convection oven to 300°F). Put the garlic cloves on a small baking sheet and roast in the oven until soft and caramelized, 50 to 60 minutes. Set aside to cool. Turn up the oven up to 375°F (convection oven to 350°F). Spread the nuts out on a baking sheet and cook in the oven until warm, 3 to 4 minutes. Let cool, then grind very coarsely using a mortar and pestle, or by pulsing in a blender.

In the meantime, peel and chop the potatoes and cook in salted boiling water until soft, 15 to 20 minutes. Drain and place in a bowl. Squeeze the soft garlic flesh out of the skins and add to the potato. Mash together until really smooth. Add the ground almonds, lemon zest and juice, a good pinch of salt, and a grinding of pepper. Stir to combine, then slowly add the olive oil in a thin stream, whisking as you do so. Check the seasoning.

To cook the lamb chops, preheat your grill, broiler, or griddle pan (oiling it lightly if necessary). Season the lamb chops generously on both sides. When hot, place the chops on the grill or griddle pan (or under the broiler) and cook for 3 minutes, then turn and cook for another 2 minutes.

Place the lamb chops on warm plates and serve with the warm spinach and skordalia.

All nuts need warming gently in the oven to release their flavor—just 3 to 4 minutes is all it takes in a preheated moderate oven to bring out their natural flavor and aroma.

Salad of lamb, green beans, and fennel with tomato and chile jam

One of the sweetest, most tender cuts of lamb is the center-cut loin. It has very little fat, so it is best cooked quickly—either sautéed or broiled. Like all meat, it should be well rested before slicing. A little feta cheese is a good addition to this salad, as a foil for the tomato and chile jam.

Serves 4

2 pieces center-cut boned lamb loin, about 3/4 pound each

sea salt and freshly ground black pepper

4 ounces fine green beans, trimmed

2 fennel bulbs, tough outer layer removed

juice of 1 lemon

olive oil, for cooking

4 handfuls of mixed salad greens

Dressing

1 tsp finely grated lemon zest

juice of 1/2 lemon, or to taste

3 tbsp extra virgin olive oil

1 1/2 tsp freshly grated Parmesan

To serve

4 tbsp Tomato and Chile Jam (toolbox, page 32)

2 tbsp black olives (optional)

Make sure the lamb is at room temperature. Bring a small pan of well-salted water to a boil, then add the green beans and blanch for 2 minutes. Drain, refresh under cold running water, and set aside. Slice the fennel very finely and immerse in a bowl of cold water with the juice of 1 lemon added to prevent discoloration.

Place a medium (preferably nonstick) skillet over medium heat and add a good splash of olive oil. Season the meat very generously with salt and pepper. When the oil is smoking, add the lamb and cook for 3 minutes on one side without moving. Then turn and cook for 2 minutes on the other side. (This will give you lamb that is pink in the center, but not bloody.) Remove from the heat, cover loosely with foil, and let it rest for 15 minutes.

While the lamb is resting, wash and pat dry the salad greens. Place in a bowl and dress with the lemon zest and juice, olive oil, and Parmesan. Season with a little salt and pepper and add a little more lemon juice if you think it is needed.

To assemble, drain the fennel and pat dry. Cut the meat into 1/2-inch-thick slices on the diagonal. Arrange the salad greens on individual plates and layer the fennel slices, beans, and lamb on top. Add a dollop of tomato and chile jam and scatter a few olives around if you like. Serve at once.

Use your favorite greens for this salad. I love the combination of beet tops, white dandelion leaves, wild arugula, basil, and mint leaves, plus sprigs of chervil— but the choice is yours.

Carrots with honey, lemon zest, and thyme

Carrots tend to be a little dull simply boiled, but cooking them with honey and butter gives them a deep, caramel flavor and thyme lends fragrance. Chestnut honey, from Italy, will impart a special taste if you can find it. The squeeze of lemon at the finish ensures that the carrots do not end up tasting disproportionately sweet.

Serves 4

8 medium carrots

1½ tbsp honey

4 tbsp unsalted butter

6 thyme sprigs

sea salt and freshly ground black pepper

grated zest and juice of ½ lemon

minced curly parsley, to sprinkle (optional)

Peel the carrots and cut them into chunky slices on the diagonal. Place in a pan and pour on enough cold water to just cover. Add the honey, butter, thyme, and a generous pinch of salt. Place over medium heat and bring to a boil, then lower the heat to a simmer. Cook for 15 minutes, or until the carrots are almost tender.

Now, turn up the heat to boil the liquid rapidly until reduced down to a shiny, sweet glaze—there should be 1 to 2 tbsp of intensely flavored cooking liquor coating the carrots … nothing more. Squeeze over the lemon juice and check the seasoning. You'll need a turn of the pepper mill and a pinch or two of salt, but no more.

Just before serving, sprinkle over the lemon zest. A scattering of minced curly parsley would not go astray either.

This simple accompaniment can be served alongside most meat, poultry, and game dishes. It goes particularly well with a simple roast chicken.

Almond panna cotta with poached tamarillos

Raw tamarillos have a very sharp flavor that is too tart for my taste, but poach them gently in a sugar syrup and they become gentler, sweeter, and much more palatable. They are jewel-like in their beauty and I can think of no prettier fruit when they are poached. Paired with smooth almond creams, they are exquisite.

Serves 4
1/2 cup blanched almonds
3/4 cup whole milk
generous 1 cup heavy cream
1/2 cup superfine sugar
1 vanilla bean, slit lengthwise
grated zest of 1 lemon
2 sheets of leaf gelatin (or
1 1/2 tsp powdered gelatin; see
toolbox, page 246)

Poached tamarillos
4 tamarillos
2 cups water
generous 1 cup superfine
sugar
1 vanilla bean, slit in half
lengthwise
1 cinnamon stick
2 bay leaves

Preheat the oven to 375°F (convection oven to 350°F). Scatter the almonds on a baking sheet and place in the oven to toast very lightly, 4 to 6 minutes. Let cool, then pulse in a food processor to chop roughly (or do this by hand).

Tip the chopped nuts into a pan and pour on the milk and cream. Add the sugar and vanilla bean and bring to a gentle simmer, stirring to help dissolve the sugar. Remove from the heat, add the lemon zest, and set aside to infuse for 15 minutes.

In the meantime, immerse the gelatin sheets in a bowl of cold water and let soften for about 5 minutes.

Return the infused almond mixture to low heat and bring just to a boil, then remove from the heat. Remove the gelatin from the bowl, squeeze out the water, then add to the hot almond cream mixture, stirring to dissolve. Strain into a pitcher, then pour into 4 individual panna cotta molds (or similar small individual molds) and let cool. Chill for about 2 hours until set, but don't leave the panna cottas in the refrigerator for too long as they will continue to firm up on chilling.

To prepare the tamarillos, cut them in half lengthwise. Put the water, sugar, vanilla, cinnamon, and bay leaves into a shallow, wide pan and place over low heat to dissolve the sugar. Then, turn up the heat and bring to a simmer. Add the tamarillos and poach for 5 to 6 minutes, or until they begin to soften and pop out of their skins. Remove from the heat and let cool in the poaching liquid.

To serve, dip the base of each mold into warm water for a second or two to loosen the edges, then invert onto a plate to turn out the panna cotta. Arrange the poached tamarillos alongside and spoon a little of the poaching syrup over them. Serve straight away.

Prune and Armagnac tart

This is a truly wonderful, classic French dessert that cannot be improved upon by any modern twists in my view. If I had to choose my last meal on Earth, this would be the dessert to round it off!

Serves 8 to 10

9 ounces Pie Dough (toolbox, page 242, 1/2 recipe)

flour, to dust

1 1/3 cups good-quality prunes, pitted

2 tbsp unsalted butter

2 organic eggs

scant 2/3 cup superfine sugar

few drops of vanilla extract

1 tbsp orange flower water

5 tbsp heavy cream

3 tbsp ground almonds

3 tbsp Armagnac, to drizzle

confectioners' sugar, to dust

crème fraîche, to serve

Roll out the pie dough on a lightly floured counter to a large circle, about 1/8 inch thick. Using your rolling pin, carefully lift the dough and drape it over a 10-inch tart pan, about 1 inch deep, with a removable bottom. Press the dough into the edges and side of the pan, using your fingers and thumbs. Trim excess dough away from the rim by rolling your pin straight across the top. Prick the base all over with a fork. Place in the refrigerator to rest for 30 minutes.

Meanwhile, preheat the oven to 375°F (convection oven to 350°F). Place the prunes in a bowl. Pour on hot water to cover and let soak for 10 minutes to soften, then drain. Melt the butter in a small pan and let cool slightly.

Line the pastry shell with waxed paper and dried beans and bake "blind" for 15 minutes. Remove the beans and paper and return to the oven until the pastry base is golden brown, about 5 minutes. Remove from the oven and let cool. Increase the oven setting to 400°F (convection oven to 375°F).

In a large bowl, combine the eggs, sugar, vanilla, orange flower water, cream, and almonds. Whisk together lightly until evenly blended, then stir in the melted butter.

Place the tart pan on a flat baking sheet (to make it easier to put in and take out of the oven). Scatter the prunes evenly over the pastry base, then ladle the egg mixture over the top. Carefully place on the middle shelf of the oven and immediately turn down the heat to 375°F (convection oven to 350°F). Bake until the custard filling is golden brown on the surface and still slightly wobbly in the center, 25 to 30 minutes.

Remove the tart from the oven and while still warm, drizzle with the Armagnac. Serve warm or at room temperature, with a dusting of confectioners' sugar and a dollop of crème fraîche.

Chocolate sorbet

Surprisingly perhaps, this icy cold, incredibly rich dessert works really well at any time of the year. It has an unforgettable silky smooth, luxurious texture. Poached kumquats are a perfect partner—their slightly sharp, citrus flavor cuts through the richness of bitter chocolate, allowing you to eat just a little bit more! These kumquats keep well in a sealed container in the refrigerator for up to 2 weeks.

Serves 8

generous 1 cup superfine sugar

2¹/2 cups water

8 ounces good-quality dark chocolate (such as Valrhona, minimum 64% cocoa solids)

1 tbsp unsweetened cocoa powder

Poached kumquats (optional)

2¹/4 pounds kumquats, washed

generous 1 cup superfine sugar

generous 1 cup water

Put the sugar and water into a pan over low heat. When the sugar has fully dissolved, bring to a boil, lower the heat slightly, and simmer for 5 minutes until the sugar syrup has a slightly viscous consistency. This is important as it helps to give the sorbet its characteristic, glossy texture.

Break up the chocolate and place in a large heatproof bowl with the cocoa. Slowly pour on the hot sugar syrup, stirring gently and continuously until the chocolate has melted into the syrup and the mixture is smooth. (The syrup will thicken considerably.) Let cool.

Once the sorbet mixture has cooled completely, pour it into your ice-cream maker and churn until thickened, according to the manufacturer's instructions. The texture should be soft.

To prepare the kumquats, cut them in half lengthwise. Tip the sugar into a pan, add the water, and dissolve over low heat, without stirring. Then, turn up the heat and cook until the syrup begins to thicken, but not yet color. Add the kumquats, lower the heat, and cook gently for 10 minutes. By now, the fruit will have softened considerably and be wonderfully glossy. Remove from the heat and let cool.

Spoon the chocolate sorbet into chilled glasses or small bowls, adding a few poached kumquats if serving.

A little Armagnac or amaretto (1 to 2 tsp) can be added before churning the mixture if you like. This will also lower the freezing temperature, resulting in an even softer, creamier sorbet.

Lemon syllabub

Wonderfully simple in its execution, this delightful dessert requires no technical skill, just willing taste buds to adjust the flavors if necessary. A little diced preserved ginger is a lovely addition if you happen to have any to hand.

Serves 8

1 cup superfine sugar

generous 3/4 cup dry sherry

finely grated zest and juice of 1 lemon

2¹/2 cups heavy cream

1 or 2 tsp minced preserved ginger in syrup (optional)

Combine the sugar, sherry, lemon zest, and juice in a bowl and stir well. In another bowl, very lightly whip the cream—just enough to thicken it slightly. Gently fold the sherry mixture into the cream until just combined (the addition of lemon and sherry will continue to thicken the cream). At this point, fold in the ginger together with a little of the syrup from the jar.

Spoon the syllabub into small glasses and refrigerate for an hour or so to chill before serving.

Poached loquats with crème fraîche

Loquats—or Japanese medlars as they are also known—are native to China and Japan and grow in the tropics and around the Mediterranean. They are delicious when cooked, but not good eaten raw. Here, I poach them in a vanilla-scented sugar syrup and serve them with crème fraîche. If you cannot find loquats, apricots (which are related) are also delicious poached in this way.

Serves 4 to 6

2¼ pounds loquats (or Japanese medlars)

generous 1 cup superfine sugar

generous 1 cup water

2 vanilla beans, slit lengthwise

finely pared zest of 1 lemon

crème fraîche, to serve

Cut each loquat in half and prize out the pit in the center. You also need to remove the fibrous skin surrounding the pit.

Put the sugar, water, vanilla beans, and lemon zest into a pan. Place over medium heat to dissolve the sugar, without stirring, then bring to a boil.

Turn down the heat to a simmer and carefully add the loquats. Poach them for 10 minutes, until they are soft and cooked through, yet still holding their shape. Remove from the heat and let cool in the sugar syrup.

Divide the loquats among glass serving bowls and spoon over some of the sugar syrup. Serve with crème fraîche.

Summer

I grew up in Australia, where summers could be fierce, with endless days on the beach and long, hot restless nights. English summers are very different, but I have learned to love them nonetheless. Gentler, sweeter, light-filled days; rich green hills; and a lazy ripe anticipation in the air.

The fresh produce during these months is absolutely glorious—strawberries, raspberries, red currants, peaches, nectarines, apricots, zucchini, summer savory, beets, peas, fava beans, wild salmon, crab, and lobster are among the finest. I love salads and at this time of year greens are at their best, especially dandelion, watercress, arugula, and wonderfully fragrant herbs including tarragon, basil, and chervil. Beautiful sweet, ripe tomatoes arrive from Italy to supplement homegrown varieties. With such a bountiful selection, to cook in summer is pure joy.

Chilled almond soup

Known as *ajo blanco* in Spain, this beautiful soup is surprisingly punchy and satisfying. I created this version for an event we shared with the Slow Food movement at Petersham in the summer of 2005, celebrating the use of flowers in the cooking of the Levant. It was, for me, a perfect day!

Serves 4

2 slices good-quality day-old bread, 1/2 inch thick

1 1/2 cups almonds

3 cloves garlic, peeled

1 1/2 tbsp sherry vinegar

generous 3/4 cup extra virgin olive oil

sea salt and freshly ground black pepper

scant 1 3/4 cups ice water (approximately)

To serve

1 perfectly ripe fig

1 tbsp rose hip syrup or extra virgin olive oil, to drizzle

1 tbsp minced parsley (optional)

Remove the crust from the bread, then cut into cubes and place in a bowl. Add cold water to cover and let soak for 2 to 3 minutes, then squeeze out excess water and set aside.

Drop the almonds into a pan of boiling water and leave for a minute or two, then remove. When cool enough to handle, slip the nuts out of their skins.

Put the garlic, almonds, bread, vinegar, and olive oil into a food processor or blender and blend until smooth. Season with salt and pepper. Then, with the motor running, slowly pour in the ice water until the soup is the thickness of heavy cream. The consistency is very important—too thick and it would feel cloying, too thin and it would be unsubstantial. Pour into a bowl, cover, and refrigerate for an hour or longer, until really well chilled.

Ladle the soup into soup plates. Cut the fig into thin wedges and lay two of these in the center of each bowl. Drizzle with a tiny amount of rose hip syrup or extra virgin olive oil if you prefer. I like to scatter over some minced parsley to serve.

Parsley soup

I love using herbs in my cooking and parsley is one of my favorites. Although it may appear old-fashioned, many of the dishes I serve are topped with parsley—chopped as finely as it possibly can be. For me, it is the perfect finish and gives a plate a delicate beauty like nothing else. Parsley takes center stage in this simple clean-tasting soup. It is an ideal start to a meal on a summer's evening.

Serves 6

2 generous bunches of curly parsley

sea salt and freshly ground black pepper

4 tbsp unsalted butter

2 leeks (white part only), well washed and chopped

1 medium-large potato, peeled and chopped

1 or 2 cloves garlic, peeled and chopped

4 cups Chicken Stock (toolbox, page 18)

2/3 cup heavy cream

Wash the bunches of parsley well—especially the stems, which can retain quite a lot of dirt. Put a large pan of well-salted water on to boil and set aside one of the parsley bunches (for blanching). Chop the other bunch roughly.

Melt the butter in another pan over low heat, then add the leeks and sweat for 2 to 3 minutes, or until starting to soften. Add the chopped parsley, along with the potato and garlic and continue to sweat for another 5 minutes. Season with salt and pepper, then pour in the chicken stock. Bring to a boil and simmer gently for 20 minutes.

Meanwhile, drop the other bunch of parsley into the pan of boiling water and blanch for 15 seconds only. Remove and immediately refresh in a bowl of ice water (to retain its intensity and give the soup a beautiful color).

When the potatoes are very tender (almost falling apart), remove the pan from the heat. In batches, purée the soup in a blender, adding some of the blanched parsley in with each batch. Blitz for a good minute or two—you want the soup to be very smooth.

Return the soup to the pan and place over medium heat. Stir in the cream, taste for seasoning, and adjust if necessary, then serve. If you have any left over, this soup will sit happily for a day or so in the refrigerator.

For a smooth finish,

you really need to use a blender to purée this soup. A food processor will not give you such a fine result. If you do not have a blender, use a food processor, then strain the soup through a chinois to ensure a smooth texture.

Spinach, fennel, and asparagus salad

I created this salad for a party given by Tate Modern to celebrate the rehanging of their permanent collections. The theme was growth and renewal, so I decided that the food should be as strong and as simple as possible—focusing on the season's beautiful produce. It was served as a course on its own, but it is also a lovely accompaniment to broiled fish. *Illustrated on previous page.*

Serves 4

5 ounces young, tender spinach leaves

1 fennel bulb

6 asparagus spears

sea salt and freshly ground black pepper

scant 1/4 cup extra virgin olive oil

finely grated zest of 1 lemon

1 tbsp finely grated Parmesan

juice of 1/2 lemon

Wash the spinach thoroughly in several charges of cold water. Place in a large pan with just the water clinging to the leaves after washing and cook over high heat until just wilted. This takes very little time—no longer than a minute—don't overcook it. Drain the spinach and set aside to cool.

To prepare the fennel, slice off the base and remove the fibrous outer leaves, then cut the bulb in half lengthwise. Place each half, cut side down, on a cutting board and cut lengthwise into fine shards, using a sharp knife—the slices should be almost paper-thin.

Snap off the woody ends of the asparagus and, using the same sharp knife, slice the spears finely lengthwise. (Shaved raw asparagus has an interesting texture and excellent taste.)

Squeeze out as much moisture from the cooled spinach as possible (but don't be so brutal that you bruise the leaves). Put the spinach into a large bowl and season with a little salt and pepper. Add the olive oil and toss through with your hands—the spinach will absorb the oil and take on a luxurious, glossy quality.

Add the fennel shards, asparagus, lemon zest, Parmesan, and lemon juice. Toss very gently with your fingertips—you want to create a feeling of space and air. Taste for seasoning, adding a little more salt if needed. Pile the salad onto plates and serve.

When I compose a salad, I like to think about every element. First I look at the season—what is around and at its best. Seasonal foods naturally work very well together. Then I think about the color, texture, and taste— bitter or sweet, gentle or peppery ... always looking to create an interesting balance.

Salad of lentils, avocado, and goat cheese

This salad really epitomizes the way I cook. It is certainly an example of how the toolbox works and of how I like to eat. I love the toolbox flavors here: the earthy, nutty lentils with a hint of sharpness from their dressing, the intense roasted tomatoes, and deep purple onions—both sweet and sharp at the same time—all brought together with the vibrant basil oil. I'm not sure whether growing up in Australia has shaped my food preferences, but I crave earthy, clean, strong flavors! Serve as an appetizer, or as a light lunch with some good peasant-style bread on the side.

Serves 4

1 cup Braised Lentils (toolbox, page 22)

2 ripe avocados

juice of 1/2 lemon

12 Slow-Roasted Tomato halves (toolbox, page 29)

7 ounces tangy, fresh goat cheese

4 ounces Roasted Red Onions (toolbox, page 29)

sea salt and freshly ground black pepper

4 tbsp Basil Oil (toolbox, page 42)

extra virgin olive oil, to drizzle

Divide the lentils among serving plates. Halve, pit, peel, and slice the avocados, then toss in the lemon juice to prevent discoloration. Layer the roasted tomatoes, goat cheese, avocado slices, and red onions on top of the lentils, alternating them and seasoning here and there with a little salt and pepper as you build. Spoon over the basil oil and finish with a drizzle of olive oil.

Vary this salad by substituting some of the ingredients. You could replace the goat cheese with a slice of broiled wild salmon or poached chicken, for example. Or add blanched asparagus or cubed roasted beets, or perhaps finely sliced celery heart, shaved fennel, or blanched green beans, or a handful of toasted nuts for crunch ... the possibilities are endless.

Peppers Piedmontese

I've prepared this dish off and on for more than 20 years, ever since I first ate it at Roger Verge's Le Moulin De Mougins in Provence with my father. It was my first Michelin 3-star experience and the most wonderful meal. In essence, it is an uncomplicated dish. I have added mozzarella, roasted onions, and basil oil, because for me, along with some good bread, it then becomes a perfect and complete lunch.

Serves 4

8 ripe tomatoes

sea salt and freshly ground black pepper

4 red bell peppers

12 basil leaves

4 cloves garlic, peeled and finely sliced

6 good-quality canned anchovies in oil, drained and cut into small pieces

2 tbsp extra virgin olive oil, to drizzle

2 balls of good-quality buffalo mozzarella or *fiore di latte* (an outstanding cow's milk mozzarella)

about 12 little black olives (ideally, Niçoise or Ligurian)

4 ounces Roasted Red Onions (toolbox, page 29)

2 tbsp Basil Oil (toolbox, page 42)

First, you need to peel the tomatoes (tedious perhaps, but necessary here). So, place a large pan of salted water on to boil. Using a small paring knife, remove the core from each tomato, then turn it upside down and mark a small cross on the base. Drop the tomatoes into the boiling water. Almost immediately (as long as the tomatoes are ripe) the skin will begin to peel back, like the petals of a flower. Remove at once with a slotted spoon and let cool slightly.

Preheat the oven to 375°F (convection oven to 350°F). Halve the bell peppers lengthwise and remove the core, seeds, and white pith. Lay the pepper halves, skin side down, in a shallow baking dish that will hold them comfortably.

When the tomatoes are cool enough, peel, halve, and remove the seeds using a teaspoon, then very roughly chop the flesh. Tear the basil leaves into pieces.

Fill the pepper halves with the pieces of tomato, garlic, basil, and anchovies. Drizzle with the olive oil and season well with pepper (not salt at this point, as the anchovies may well provide all that is needed). Bake in the oven until the peppers are soft and slightly blackened around the edges, but still holding their shape, 25 to 35 minutes.

Check the seasoning and let the roasted peppers cool—room temperature is the ideal warmth to really appreciate the summery flavors of this dish.

Arrange the peppers on a big oval plate so everybody can help themselves, or on individual plates if you prefer. Tear the mozzarella into pieces with your hands and scatter over the peppers, along with the olives and roasted red onions. Spoon over the basil oil to serve.

Eggplants are at their best during the summer months, although you can buy them throughout the year. Look for eggplants with firm, glossy skins that feel heavy in the hand.

Baked eggplants with tomatoes, tarragon, and crème fraîche

I love this dish because it sings of summer. Served just warm with nutty brown rice, garlicky yogurt, and an arugula salad on the side, it makes a lovely vegetarian supper. It also works well with broiled or barbecued lamb.

Serves 4 to 6

3 globe eggplants, about 1 pound each, trimmed

sea salt and freshly ground black pepper

olive oil, to pan-fry

4 tbsp unsalted butter

2 1/4 pounds ripe tomatoes, roughly chopped

4 cloves garlic, peeled and sliced

1 3/4 cups crème fraîche

2 tbsp tarragon leaves, minced

2 tbsp chopped Italian parsley, plus extra to finish

1/2 tbsp chopped thyme leaves (ideally, lemon thyme), plus sprigs to garnish

1 tbsp minced chives

2 ounces Parmesan, freshly grated

extra virgin olive oil, to drizzle

Slice the eggplants into 1/2-inch circles. Lay in a colander and sprinkle generously with salt. Let degorge the bitter juices for about 30 minutes—beads of moisture will appear on the eggplant flesh. Before cooking, pat each eggplant slice dry with paper towels.

Heat a 1/2-inch depth of olive oil in a large, fairly deep skillet over medium-high heat. Pan-fry the eggplant slices, a few at a time, until golden brown on one side, then turn and brown on the other side. Remove and drain on paper towels.

Melt the butter in another pan. Add the tomatoes and garlic and season with a good pinch of salt and some pepper. Cook over low heat for about 15 minutes, until the tomatoes are soft.

Meanwhile, put the crème fraîche into a small pan and bring to a boil over medium heat. Let bubble until reduced by a third, then remove from the heat and add the tarragon, parsley, thyme, and chives. Add half of the Parmesan and taste for seasoning.

Preheat the oven to 375°F (convection oven to 350°F). Line the bottom of a large, shallow ovenproof baking dish with a layer of eggplant slices. Follow with a thin coating of the tomato sauce and a sprinkling of the remaining Parmesan. Continue layering in this way, finishing with tomato sauce. Pour over the crème fraîche mixture and sprinkle with the remaining Parmesan. Let the dish sit for a few minutes to allow the flavors to get acquainted with each other.

Place in the oven and bake until golden brown, 16 to 20 minutes. Let stand for 5 minutes or so. Drizzle with a little extra virgin olive oil and sprinkle with a pinch or two of salt. Scatter over some minced parsley and thyme sprigs to garnish and serve … but not too hot!

Braised artichokes with fennel, tomatoes, olives, and preserved lemon

This is a vegetable dish that really holds its own. It is a lovely way to serve globe artichokes, which are a summertime vegetable in the UK. Deeply nourishing, with sage lending warm base note tones, it is a perfect dish for a cooler summer's evening.

Serves 4

2 heads of fennel

1 lemon, halved

1 tbsp olive oil

2 tbsp unsalted butter

sea salt and freshly ground black pepper

2 globe artichokes

2 bay leaves

3 tsp chopped sage, plus extra leaves to garnish

2 cloves garlic, peeled and minced

1 dried red chile

small pinch of saffron threads

4 good-quality ripe tomatoes (preferably plum), roughly chopped

1/2 preserved lemon, chopped

generous 1/3 cup Chicken Stock (toolbox, page 18)

about 12 little black olives (ideally, Niçoise or Ligurian)

2 tbsp Basil Oil (toolbox, page 42), or to taste

freshly grated Parmesan, to serve

Preheat the oven to 375°F (convection oven to 350°F). Trim the fennel and cut off the base, then remove the fibrous outer layer. Cut each fennel bulb into quarters and squeeze over a little lemon juice.

Place a heavy ovenproof pan over medium heat, add the olive oil and butter, and heat until the butter has melted. Add the fennel, season with a little salt, and cook for 10 minutes.

Meanwhile, prepare the artichokes—a sharp knife is imperative. Lay each artichoke on its side on a cutting board, then cut off the top third and discard. Cut off the stalk and trim all the way around the base until you come to the choke—you should now be left with just the heart. Cut the artichoke heart in half and, with a small paring knife, remove the spiky, fibrous inner choke. Quickly rub the artichoke hearts with the cut lemon to prevent discoloration.

Add the artichoke hearts to the fennel along with the bay leaves, sage, and garlic. Crumble in the dried chile and saffron and stir to combine. Add the tomatoes to the pan, along with the preserved lemon, then pour in the chicken stock. Cover and cook in the oven until the fennel is very tender, 30 to 40 minutes, adding the olives for the last 5 minutes.

Taste and adjust the seasoning, then spoon over the basil oil and scatter over some sage leaves to garnish. Sprinkle with grated Parmesan and serve.

Tea-smoked fillets of wild salmon with pickled cucumber salad

Tea-smoking works really well with all oily fish, but especially with salmon—the delicate flavors complement each other perfectly. For smoking, I like to use a fragrant heady tea, such as Lapsang or Yunnan, but experiment to find out which ones you like best. The salmon can be tea-smoked the day before and kept overnight in the refrigerator if that's more convenient.

Serves 4

1 recipe Tea-Smoking Mixture (toolbox, page 20)

4 wild salmon fillets, about 6 ounces each

Cucumber salad

1 large cucumber, peeled and finely sliced on the diagonal

2 tsp sea salt

Dressing

juice of 2 limes

1$^{1}/_{2}$ tsp sugar

1 tbsp fish sauce

1 tbsp chopped cilantro leaves

1 tbsp minced mint leaves

1 clove garlic, peeled and minced

1 fresh red chile, seeded and finely diced

2 drops of toasted sesame oil

To serve

1 recipe Mayonnaise (toolbox, page 36)

Prepare the tea-smoking mixture and set up the tea-smoking equipment as described in the toolbox. Tea-smoke the salmon fillets according to the toolbox instructions, cooking them for 3 minutes. Turn off the heat and let the salmon sit in the baking pan with the lid on until cooked, for another 3 to 4 minutes. Remove the lid, take out the fish, and set aside until ready to serve.

For the salad, sprinkle the cucumber with the salt, tossing gently with your fingers to distribute evenly. Place the slices in a colander and let stand for an hour.

To make the dressing, whisk together all the ingredients, except the sesame oil, in a bowl. Whisk in the sesame oil.

Rinse the cucumber slices very lightly under cool water and pat dry with a clean, dry dish towel. Place in a bowl, drizzle over the dressing, and toss gently to combine.

Place the tea-smoked salmon fillets on serving plates and pile the cucumber salad alongside. Pass the mayonnaise around separately in a bowl.

Crab claws with chile oil and mayonnaise

This is hardly a recipe at all—just a combination of delicious things to share! I love food that you have to work a little harder at to eat—it creates a sense of congeniality and community—shared food in the middle of the table is my preferred way of eating. A good fish supplier will be happy to provide you with beautiful, freshly cooked crab claws.

Serves 4

12 to 16 freshly cooked crab claws (3 to 4 per person)

1 recipe Chile Oil (toolbox, page 44)

1 recipe Mayonnaise (toolbox, page 36)

1 or 2 lemons, cut into wedges (for squeezing over the crab)

little bowls of sea salt

basket of chewy peasant-style bread

small bowl of radishes (optional)

Crack the crab claws gently with the back of a heavy knife, without crushing the meat. Pile them onto a platter. Place in the middle of the table, along with all the other ingredients. Provide finger bowls for everyone, too. Bon appétit!

Beautiful bread is a very important part of any meal, though it has its place. Offering a large basket at the beginning of a meal encourages people to fill up too early, lessening their enjoyment of the food to follow, so try to bear this in mind. Choose breads with character—open textured with a chewy crust. I particularly like sourdoughs and ryes— breads that hold their own and add their particular dimension to a meal.

Squid and chorizo with black olives and red pepper

This lovely inky, unctuous stew is very satisfying to eat, especially when served with garlicky, chewy toast. I have at different times varied the ingredients, adding large cubes of potato, blanched kale, or spinach, even substituting the chorizo with mussels or clams. A dollop of saffron mayonnaise or a spoonful of lemon-infused or basil oil stirred in at the end gives the dish a wonderful vibrancy.

Serves 6

2¹/4 pounds baby squid

14 ounces chorizo sausage

4 tbsp olive oil

1 yellow onion, peeled and diced

2 carrots, peeled and finely diced

1 celery stalk, diced

3 cloves garlic, peeled and crushed

3 thyme sprigs

4 bay leaves

1 small dried red chile

sea salt and freshly ground black pepper

finely pared zest of 1 orange

1 red bell pepper, halved, cored, seeded, and cut into strips

1¹/2 cups red wine

1 (14-ounce) can good-quality chopped tomatoes

12 to 18 little black olives (ideally, Niçoise or Ligurian)

To serve

6 slices of chewy peasant-style bread

1 clove garlic, halved

Clean the squid by pulling the tentacles and head from the body. Cut the tentacles from the head, discarding the head. Remove the transparent quill from the body and the soft, gooey matter. Rinse the body pouch and tentacles gently under cold running water, drain, and set aside. Slice the chorizo on the diagonal into 1/2-inch-thick slices.

Heat 3 tbsp of the olive oil in a deep, heavy pan. Add the onion, carrots, celery, garlic, thyme, and bay leaves. Crumble in the dried chile and season with a good pinch of sea salt. Twist the orange zest with your fingers (to release its fragrance) and drop into the pan. Cover and sweat over very low heat for 15 minutes, stirring occasionally. Add the bell pepper and sweat for another 5 minutes.

Pour in the wine and turn up the heat so that it bubbles and reduces slightly. Add the tomatoes, stir well, and cook uncovered for 10 minutes. The idea is to reduce the sauce and intensify the flavor.

Meanwhile, heat the remaining 1 tbsp olive oil in a skillet. When smoking, add the chorizo slices and brown quickly on both sides. Tip straight into the tomato mixture, along with the orange, smoky-flavored oil. Add the olives and simmer for a minute or two. Check the seasoning—you will probably need just a little black pepper and perhaps a small pinch or two of salt, just to bring it all together.

Pour off excess oil from the skillet, then place over high heat. In small batches, quickly brown the squid in the very hot pan for no more than a minute, then drop them straight into the inky stew.

Turn off the heat while you toast the bread on both sides. Rub the toast slices with the cut garlic clove. Ladle the stew into warm bowls, discarding the herbs and orange zest. Serve straight away, with the hot garlicky toast.

Red mullet with fennel and saffron mayonnaise

Red mullet is a highly prized fish pulled from the Mediterranean. It should be vibrant rosy pink in color—shot through with gold flecks. If unavailable, you can use small red snapper, ocean perch, or striped bass instead. Ask your fish supplier to clean the fish for you.

Serves 4

8 small red mullet, or
4 medium ones

5 black peppercorns, crushed

1 orange, halved

4 bay leaves, plus extra to garnish if you like

generous 3/4 cup extra virgin olive oil

3 small, smooth fennel bulbs

4 tbsp unsalted butter

sea salt and freshly ground black pepper

juice of 1 lemon

To serve

Saffron Mayonnaise (toolbox, page 36)

Place the fish side by side in a dish and prick the skin here and there with a needle. Sprinkle with the peppercorns and squeeze over the orange juice. Add the bay leaves and pour over 1/2 cup of the olive oil. Cover and let marinate for 3 to 4 hours in a cool place (preferably not the refrigerator).

Trim the fennel and cut into quarters. Roughly chop a few of the feathery fronds and set aside. Melt the butter in a sauté pan. When it is foaming, add the fennel and season with a little salt and pepper. Sweat gently for 3 minutes, then add the lemon juice.

Add water to cover and turn up the heat until the liquor is bubbling. Pour in the remaining 1/4 cup olive oil and cook for about 15 minutes, until the fennel is really tender and the liquor is well reduced. Check the seasoning and set aside.

Remove the fish from the dish, reserving the marinade, and pat dry. Season with salt and pepper.

Heat 3 tbsp of the marinade in a large skillet. When hot, add the fish (you will probably need to cook them in two batches). Allow 2 minutes on each side for little mullet, about 3 minutes on each side for larger fish (it is important that they remain moist).

To serve, divide the fennel among warm plates and lay the fish on top. Add a dollop of saffron mayonnaise or pass around separately in a bowl. Sprinkle with a little chopped fennel frond and garnish each plate with a sprig of bay leaves if you like. Serve at once.

Monkfish and clams with roasted almonds, rosemary, and aïoli

In France, monkfish is known as poor man's lobster. Plump, white, and firm, with only a backbone, it is easy to fillet and its meaty texture works well in fish stews. Here you can use mussels or shrimp instead of clams, perhaps adding a handful of black olives, or leaving out the almonds … it's up to you. I serve it with garlicky sourdough toast and a leafy salad dressed with lemon and olive oil.

Serves 4

4 tbsp olive oil

2 large red onions, peeled and thinly sliced

sea salt and freshly ground black pepper

about 25 saffron threads

generous 1 cup boiling water

2 fennel bulbs

2 dried red chiles

4 rosemary sprigs

2 bay leaves

4 cloves garlic, peeled and minced

1 tbsp sherry vinegar

generous 1 cup dry white wine

2 (14-ounce) cans good-quality chopped tomatoes

1/2 cup blanched almonds

2 1/4 pounds monkfish, skinned, filleted, and cut into generous chunks

40 clams, scrubbed clean

To serve

4 slices of sourdough bread

1 clove garlic, halved

Aïoli (toolbox, page 36) or Rosemary and Almond Aïoli (page 221)

Heat the olive oil in a large heavy pan over medium-low heat, then add the onions with a pinch of salt and cook gently for about 5 minutes, until soft. Put the saffron in a small bowl, pour on the boiling water, and let infuse. Preheat the oven to 375°F (convection oven to 350°F).

In the meantime, prepare the fennel. Slice off the base and remove the fibrous outer leaves, then finely slice lengthwise and add to the onions. Crumble in the dried chiles and add the rosemary, bay leaves, and garlic. Cook for another 10 minutes, until the fennel has started to soften.

Add the vinegar, wine, and saffron together with its water. Allow the liquor to bubble away for a couple of minutes, then add the tomatoes. Give the mixture a good stir, turn down the heat, and cook gently for 20 minutes. The flavors need time to adjust to each other.

In the meantime, lightly toast the almonds on a baking sheet in the oven for 3 to 4 minutes to release their flavor. Coarsely grind the toasted nuts, using a mortar and pestle, or blender.

Stir the nuts into the tomato mixture—they give the dish a lovely textural quality as well as a delicious nutty flavor. Check the seasoning … you will definitely need to add salt and pepper. (The dish can be prepared ahead to this point.)

About 5 minutes before serving, bring the tomato mixture to a boil. Add the monkfish and clams and simmer for 4 minutes, or until the clams have opened and the monkfish is firm to the touch and white in color. Discard the herbs and any clams that have not opened.

Meanwhile, toast the bread on both sides and rub with the cut garlic clove. Serve the fish stew with the toast, a bowl of garlicky aïoli, and a simple salad.

Buy shellfish as
close as possible to
cooking and keep cool.
Mussels and clams are
happiest immersed
in a bowl of well-salted
water in the refrigerator
until you are ready to
cook them.

Pan-roasted chicken with lentils, roasted tomatoes, and basil oil

I always think that chicken supremes with the wing tips attached taste better... and you have the added pleasure of being able to gnaw on the bone. Don't be put off at first glance by the number of toolbox components in this recipe—remember that just about every item in the toolbox lasts well in the refrigerator for up to a week.

Serves 4

2 cups Braised Lentils (toolbox, page 22)

generous 1 cup Chicken Stock (toolbox, page 18)

2 tbsp tamari or soy sauce

4 organic chicken supremes (bone-in, skin-on breasts with the first wing joint attached)

sea salt and freshly ground black pepper

1 tbsp olive oil

8 to 12 Slow-Roasted Tomato halves (toolbox, page 29)

2 tbsp Basil Oil (toolbox, page 42)

4 tbsp Aïoli (toolbox, page 36)

minced curly parsley, to finish

Preheat the oven to 425°F (convection oven to 400°F). Place the lentils in a pan, pour over the chicken stock, and bring to a boil. Turn down the heat, add the tamari, and simmer for 2 minutes. Keep warm.

Meanwhile, season the chicken supremes with salt and pepper. Place a large ovenproof (preferably nonstick) pan over high heat. Add the olive oil and when it is hot and just starting to smoke, lcarefully ay the chicken breasts in the pan, skin side down. Cook without moving (resist the temptation) for 4 minutes, until the skin is golden brown. Without turning the supremes, put the pan into the oven (or you could transfer them to a large roasting pan). Roast, skin side down, until the chicken breasts feel firm when you press with your fingers, 6 to 8 minutes. Remove from the oven and let rest in a warm place for 5 minutes or so.

Divide the warm lentils among warm plates. Place a few roasted tomatoes and a chicken supreme on top of each portion and drizzle the basil oil over the lentils. Add a dollop of garlicky aïoli (or pass around separately in a bowl if you prefer). Finish with a sprinkling of minced parsley.

The most vital
ingredient in
any dish is the
attitude you bring to
it. Love and passion
make for a happy
cook ... and food
with soul.

Vitello tonnato with tomatoes, olives, and basil oil

Vitello tonnato is a classic Italian dish—perfect on a summer menu. It works equally well as a simple one-course lunch or as part of a buffet. Its beauty lies in the contrast of the sweet, delicate veal against the creamy intense sauce. I've seen other meats used in place of veal, but I don't think anything else works as well. The meat is poached rather than roasted, to keep it moist and tender.

Serves 6 to 8

Poached veal

3 pounds veal top round

1 yellow onion, peeled and quartered

3 celery stalks, chopped

2 carrots, peeled and chopped

4 bay leaves

small bunch of Italian parsley

8 to 10 peppercorns

Tuna mayonnaise

generous 3/4 cup Mayonnaise (toolbox, page 36)

1 (7-ounce) can fine-quality tuna, drained

2 tbsp lemon juice

2 tbsp capers (packed in salt), well rinsed and drained

3 fine-quality canned anchovy fillets in olive oil, drained

freshly ground black pepper

To assemble

3 ripe tomatoes

2 handfuls of arugula leaves

lemon juice

olive oil

2 tbsp little black olives (ideally, Niçoise or Ligurian)

1 tbsp capers, rinsed and drained

3 tbsp Basil Oil (toolbox, page 42)

Half-fill a cooking pot or heavy pan (large enough to hold the veal) with water. Add the onion, celery, carrots, bay leaves, parsley, and peppercorns (but no salt). Bring the water to a boil, then add the veal. There should be sufficient water to cover the meat—if not, add enough to do so. Turn down the heat to a steady, gentle simmer and cook for 1 1/2 hours. Remove the pan from the heat and let the veal cool completely in the stock (this helps keep it moist).

Meanwhile, prepare the tuna mayonnaise. Put the tuna into a food processor along with the lemon juice, capers, and anchovy fillets. Add the mayonnaise and process until you have a smooth sauce. Taste for seasoning—the sauce will benefit from a grinding or two of black pepper, but is unlikely to need any salt (as anchovies and capers are both salty). Set aside.

When ready to serve, lift the meat out of the cold stock and place it on a cutting board. Snip off any string and slice the meat with a sharp knife as finely as possible. Cut the tomatoes into big, uneven chunks. Dress the arugula with a squeeze of lemon juice and a few drops of olive oil.

Layer the veal slices on a platter with the tomatoes and arugula. Spoon the tuna mayonnaise on top of the veal, scatter over the olives and capers, and drizzle over the basil oil. Serve at once, with some good bread.

Roast chicken and bread salad with sour cherries and roasted red onions

I love torn bread salads—the trick is to combine the salad while the bread is still warm, so it can absorb and take on all the flavors. Here, a freshly cooked bird with real flavor is essential—last night's roast chicken will not do. You can replace the chicken with finely sliced prosciutto or, for a meat-free version, lace the bread generously with sweet broiled red bell peppers and black olives.

Serves 4 to 6

Roast chicken

1 small organic chicken, about 3 pounds

1 lemon, halved

1 small bunch of thyme

2 bay leaves

small bunch of parsley

5 cloves garlic, halved

1 dried red chile, crumbled

olive oil, to drizzle

sea salt and freshly ground black pepper

Salad

2 tbsp dried sour cherries (or cranberries or raisins)

1 loaf of 1-day-old chewy peasant-style bread

about 2/3 cup extra virgin olive oil

1/3 cup Roasted Red Onions (toolbox, page 29)

1 tbsp salted capers, rinsed

1 tbsp minced preserved lemon

2 tbsp saba or good-quality balsamic vinegar

large handful of arugula leaves

2 or 3 tbsp Basil Oil (toolbox, page 42)

finely grated zest of 1 lemon

Preheat the oven to 425°F (convection oven to 400°F). Rinse the chicken inside and out and remove the little fat deposits just inside the cavity. Pat dry. Put one lemon half into the cavity along with the thyme, bay leaves, parsley, garlic, and dried chile. Squeeze the juice from the other lemon half over the chicken skin, then drizzle with olive oil, massaging it into the skin with your fingers. Season generously with salt and pepper.

Place the chicken in a roasting pan and roast for 15 minutes, then lower the oven setting to 375°F (convection oven to 350°F) and roast until cooked through, 35 to 45 minutes. To test, pierce the thickest part of the thigh with a skewer—the juices should run clear. Let rest in a warm place until cool enough to handle. Pour off the fat from the roasting pan, saving the juices. Leave the oven on.

For the salad, soak the sour cherries in warm water to cover for 10 minutes. Cut the loaf in half lengthwise and tear with your hands into pieces, roughly 1 1/4 to 1 1/2 inches square. Spread the bread pieces out on a baking sheet and drizzle with 2 tbsp of the olive oil. Bake in the oven until golden brown, 8 to 10 minutes.

Tip the bread into a large salad bowl. While it is still warm, drizzle over the remaining olive oil, adjusting the quantity as necessary—the bread should not feel dry. Add the roasted red onions, capers, preserved lemon, and saba or balsamic vinegar . Toss together with your hands. Drain the cherries and pat dry, then add to the salad.

When the chicken is cool enough to handle, tear the flesh off the bones and cut into bite-size pieces. Add to the salad and drizzle over the roasting juices. Toss the chicken through, then add the arugula and toss again. Check the seasoning.

Pile the salad into a serving dish, drizzle over the basil oil, and sprinkle with lemon zest. Serve straight away, while still just warm.

Rare roast beef salad with green beans, new potatoes, and horseradish cream

This tempting salad is a complete meal in itself—perfect for a weekend lunch. The accompanying horseradish cream has a definite kick to it, though you could reduce the grated horseradish for a milder flavor if you prefer.

Serves 4

13/4 pounds best-quality beef tenderloin

sea salt and freshly ground black pepper

1 tbsp olive oil

1¹/3 pounds little new potatoes (La Ratte or other fingerling potato)

2¹/2 cups haricot verts, trimmed

grated zest and juice of ¹/2 lemon

2 tbsp extra virgin olive oil

handful of mixed salad greens (such as young red chard and dandelion)

1 tbsp freshly grated Parmesan

8 to 12 Slow-Roasted Tomato halves (toolbox, page 29)

²/3 cup Roasted Red Onions (toolbox, page 29)

2 tbsp Basil Oil (toolbox, page 42)

Horseradish cream

3/4 cup crème fraîche

3 tbsp freshly grated horseradish

1 tbsp Dijon mustard

sea salt

Start by making the horseradish cream. Put the crème fraîche into a bowl and add the horseradish and mustard. Stir to combine and season with a pinch of salt to bring out the flavor of the horseradish. Set aside.

Preheat the oven to 425°F (convection oven to 400°F). Trim the meat of any sinew and fat, then season generously all over with salt and pepper. Heat a heavy ovenproof skillet over high heat, then add the 1 tbsp olive oil. When smoking, add the beef and sear to color on all sides. Transfer the skillet to the oven and roast until cooked rare, or 12 minutes. Cover loosely with foil and set aside to rest for 20 minutes.

In the meantime, cook the potatoes in boiling salted water until tender, 10 to 15 minutes. Bring another pan of salted water to a boil, add the green beans, and blanch for 2 minutes. Drain and refresh in cold water, then pat dry with a clean cloth. Drain the potatoes as soon as they are cooked and cut in half lengthwise.

Put the warm potatoes in a bowl, season with a little salt and pepper, and dress with the lemon zest, lemon juice, and extra virgin olive oil. Let cool, then add the salad greens and green beans. Toss lightly with your hands and sprinkle with the Parmesan.

Slice the beef into ¹/4-inch-thick slices. Layer the beef slices and salad on serving plates, piling it high, and add 2 or 3 roasted tomato halves, some roasted red onions, and a spoonful of horseradish cream to each plate. Finally, drizzle the basil oil over the top and serve.

Fava beans and peas with mint and feta

This is really a little summer side dish. It works well with roasted chicken at room temperature, served with a properly ripe tomato salad and crusty bread on the side. It is also delicious with barbecued butterflied leg of lamb or broiled steaks, but for me, only when the weather is warm. To my mind, it is a dish best eaten outside.

Serves 4

generous 1 cup freshly podded fava beans

sea salt and freshly ground black pepper

generous 1 cup freshly podded peas

small bunch of mint (leaves only)

juice of 1/2 lemon

1/4 cup extra virgin olive oil

6 ounces barrel-aged Greek feta or other good-quality feta cheese

1/3 cup Roasted Red Onions (toolbox, page 29)

2 tbsp Basil Oil, or to taste (toolbox, page 42)

finely grated zest of 1/2 lemon, or to taste

Bring a large pan of well-salted water to a boil. Add the fava beans, allow the water to come back to a boil, and cook for 45 seconds. Remove with a slotted spoon to a colander and refresh under cold water. When cool, slip off the dull greenish gray skins to reveal the limey green beans inside and place these in a bowl.

To blanch the peas, drop them into the same boiling water, return to a boil, and cook for 1 minute. Drain and refresh under cold running water, then pat dry and add to the fava beans.

Tear the mint and toss through the peas and fava beans. Squeeze over the lemon juice and drizzle with the olive oil. Toss to combine and season with a grinding of pepper and perhaps the tiniest amount of salt (if any at all, as the feta will be intensely salty).

Slice the feta into long fine shards, or crumble it between your fingers if you prefer. Pile the salad into serving bowls and surround with the feta. Spoon the roasted onions over the salad. Drizzle with basil oil and sprinkle with lemon zest to serve.

Double podding fava beans may seem a bit tedious, but it transforms them from tough, dull vegetables into tender beans that are beautiful to look at and a treat to eat.

Sweet potato and goat cheese frittata

This frittata often appears as a very thin slice on our mezze plate. I love to eat it on its own though, with a simple herby green salad, like the one we serve with the mezze (see page 69). You can make it all year round—sweet potatoes are more of a fall vegetable—but to me it is a summery dish, not least because it is perfect picnic food. Use the best-quality organic, free-range eggs that you can find—their flavor will make all the difference. I prefer the taste of this frittata at room temperature, when the flavors are clearer, but of course you can serve it warm if you prefer.

Serves 4

1 medium sweet potato
(or 2 small ones)

sea salt and freshly ground
black pepper

9 ounces fresh, young rindless
goat cheese

1/2 cup Roasted Red Onions
(toolbox, page 29)

5 tbsp Basil Oil (toolbox, page
42)

2 1/4 ounces Parmesan, freshly
grated

10 organic eggs

1 tbsp olive oil

Preheat the oven to 350°F (convection oven to 325°F). Peel the sweet potato, cut into chunks, and place in a pan. Cover with cold water, add a pinch of salt, and bring to a boil. Lower the heat and simmer until tender, about 15 minutes. Drain and tip into a large bowl.

While the sweet potato is still warm, crumble the goat cheese into the bowl. Toss in the roasted red onions, spoon over the basil oil, and sprinkle with the Parmesan. Toss together lightly and set aside.

Break the eggs into a separate bowl and season generously with salt and plenty of pepper. Whisk to combine.

Place an 8- to 10-inch ovenproof (preferably nonstick) skillet over medium heat and add the olive oil. When the pan is hot, add the sweet potato and goat cheese mixture, distributing it evenly over the bottom of the pan. Pour in the beaten egg and, using a fork, tease it in between the sweet potato chunks, making sure it gets into all the nooks and crannies.

Lower the heat and cook gently for 3 to 4 minutes, then transfer the skillet to the oven and cook until firm on the surface but still slightly soft and runny in the center, or until set, 9 to 10 minutes. The frittata will continue to firm up as it cools out of the oven.

Spinach with garlic, lemon, and chile

I love all vegetables (with the possible exception of okra), but spinach is the one that I am totally devoted to. To me, it is equally appealing eaten hot or at room temperature, and I often crave a mouthful of its inky goodness. This side dish goes with many things, but I particularly like it with simple broiled white fish and pan-fried veal or chicken.

Serves 4

2¹/4 pounds spinach (preferably young leaves)

4 tbsp extra virgin olive oil

2 cloves garlic, peeled and sliced

¹/2 medium fresh red chile, seeded and finely sliced

sea salt and freshly ground black pepper

juice of ¹/4 lemon

Wash your spinach really well in a couple of changes of cold water. If using young spinach, there is no need to remove the stems. If using bigger spinach leaves, cut out the slightly tough central stem. Shake the leaves dry.

Cook the spinach in several batches in a large sauté pan over medium-high heat with just the water clinging to the leaves after washing until only just wilted, then drain in a colander to remove excess liquid. Wipe the pan dry.

Heat the olive oil in the sauté pan over medium-high heat and add the garlic and chile. Tip the spinach into the pan and add a generous pinch of salt. Toss to mix—the spinach will look vibrant and glossy with its coating of olive oil.

Squeeze over the lemon juice and add a grinding or two of pepper. Serve immediately.

Meringues with summer fruits and crème anglaise

This dessert is only really wonderful when your fruit is perfect. Don't be tempted to try and re-create it out of summer with fruit that has been flown halfway around the world. Savor it during the summer months using beautiful, fragrant summer berries and perfectly ripe nectarines.

Serves 8

Meringues
6 organic egg whites (at room temperature)
pinch of salt
generous 13/4 cups superfine sugar
3/4 tsp vanilla extract

Crème anglaise
2 cups whole milk
2/3 cup heavy cream
1 vanilla bean, split lengthwise
scant 2/3 cup superfine sugar
6 organic egg yolks

To assemble
4 nectarines
13/4 cups strawberries
1 cup raspberries
confectioners' sugar, to dust

For the meringues, preheat the oven to 325°F (convection oven to 300°F). Line a baking sheet with parchment paper. Make the meringue, following the method in the dessert toolbox (page 244). It should be stiff and glossy. Using a large serving spoon, shape 8 generous mounds of meringue on the baking sheet, spacing them well apart to allow room for expansion. Place in the oven and immediately turn down the setting to 275°F (convection oven to 250°F). Cook for 45 to 50 minutes. Turn off the heat and let the meringues cool completely in the oven before removing, they should be crisp.

To make the crème anglaise, put the milk and cream in a heavy pan with the vanilla bean and place over medium heat. Bring to a simmer, then immediately remove from the heat, cover, and let infuse for 20 minutes.

Whisk together the sugar and egg yolks in a heatproof bowl for a minute or two until the mixture is slightly paler in color. Return the cream to low heat to warm through. When it is just hot, pour onto the yolk mixture, stirring with the whisk as you do so.

Pour the custard back into the pan and place back on the lowest possible heat. Now a little patience is required. Take a wooden spoon and using a figure-eight motion, stir continuously until the custard thickens enough to cling to the back of the spoon. This may take as long as 10 minutes. (Don't be tempted to turn up the heat, or the eggs may well scramble.) When you have the correct consistency, remove from the heat, strain the custard through a fine strainer into a cold bowl, and set aside to cool to room temperature. Then cover and place in the refrigerator to chill thoroughly.

When ready to serve, halve the nectarines, prize out the pits, and cut the flesh into thin slices. Hull most of the strawberries and cut in half lengthwise, leaving a few with their stalks on for decoration. Combine with the raspberries and nectarine slices.

Pour a generous pool of chilled custard onto each serving plate and place a meringue in the center. Pile the fruit next to the meringue, dust with confectioners' sugar, and serve straight away.

Raspberry and apricot bread puddings

I must confess that I love bread and butter pudding. There is something so comforting about the soft, velvety taste of homemade custard laced with specks of vanilla, contrasting with the sugary crunch of the golden bread topping. Here, apricots and raspberries lend a slightly lemony, not too sweet, summery taste that makes the pudding feel a touch less indulgent ... than in fact it probably is!

Serves 8

unsalted butter, to grease

8 fresh apricots

generous 1/3 cup superfine sugar, plus 1 1/2 tbsp

1 tbsp apricot liqueur (or amaretto)

4 organic eggs

1 tsp vanilla extract

1 1/4 cups heavy cream

1 1/4 cups whole milk

8 thin slices of white bread, crusts removed

1 1/4 cups raspberries

confectioners' sugar, to dust

half-and-half, to serve

Preheat the oven to 325°F (convection oven to 300°F). Lightly grease 8 individual ovenproof ramekins or custard cups, 2/3-cup capacity, with butter.

Halve the apricots, remove the pits, and chop the flesh into small cubes. Place in a bowl and sprinkle with the 1 1/2 tbsp sugar. Drizzle over the liqueur and let macerate while you make the custard base.

Put the 1/3 cup sugar and the eggs in a bowl along with the vanilla and whisk together until pale and creamy. Add the heavy cream and milk, stir to combine, and pass through a fine strainer into a pitcher.

Layer the bread slices with the raspberries and macerated apricots in the prepared ramekins, trimming the bread to fit as necessary. Pour over the custard and let stand for 15 minutes.

Place the ramekins in a large baking dish and pour in enough water to come halfway up the sides of the ramekins. Carefully place in the oven and bake until golden and the custard is set, 25 to 30 minutes.

Serve the puddings warm or, better still, at room temperature. To unmold, run a knife around the inside of the dishes and turn out the puddings onto plates. Dust with confectioners' sugar just before serving. Pass around a pitcher of half-and-half.

Almond tart with blackberries

I find the simplicity of this dessert very appealing. It is merely a pastry shell filled with the classic French frangipane and fresh fruit. You can make it all year round, adapting the fruit to the seasons— plums and quinces in fall, apples and pears in winter, apricots when they appear in spring. My favorite way to eat it is in the afternoon, accompanied by an espresso coffee and nothing else!

Serves 8 to 10

9 ounces Pie Dough (toolbox, page 242, 1/2 recipe)

flour, to dust

1 1/3 cups blanched almonds

1 cup superfine sugar

scant 1 cup unsalted butter, at room temperature

1 tsp vanilla extract

6 organic egg yolks

13/4 cups blackberries

crème fraîche, to serve

Roll out the pie dough on a lightly floured counter to a large circle, about 1/8 inch thick. Using your rolling pin, carefully lift the dough and drape it over a 10-inch tart pan, about 1 inch deep, with a removable bottom. Press the dough into the edges and side of the pan, using your fingers and thumbs. Trim excess dough away from the rim by rolling your pin straight across the top. Prick the base here and there with a fork. Refrigerate for 20 minutes.

Meanwhile, preheat the oven to 375°F (convection oven to 350°F). Line the pastry shell with waxed paper and dried beans and bake "blind" for 15 minutes. Remove the beans and paper and return to the oven until the pastry base is golden brown, about 5 minutes. Remove from the oven and let cool. Leave the oven on.

For the almond filling, spread the nuts out on a baking sheet and warm in the oven for 3 to 4 minutes. Leave the oven on. Let cool, then grind very coarsely using a mortar and pestle, or by pulsing in a blender.

Cream together the sugar and butter in a bowl, using an electric mixer until smooth and pale, then add the vanilla. Add the egg yolks, one at a time, whisking until just combined, then incorporate the almonds.

Pour the almond filling into the pastry shell, then stud evenly all over with the blackberries. Bake until the filling is golden brown, 25 to 30 minutes. Set aside to cool.

Serve the tart at room temperature, with crème fraîche.

Strawberry granita

This is my favorite granita of all. It reminds me of my teenage years in Sydney, as I would often make a detour with friends to the Roma café, where strawberry granita was served in a macchiato glass with fresh cream poured over the top. We would eat this mouthwatering summer treat accompanied by an espresso and think we were very grown up. I still love the pure, clean explosion of iced strawberry in my mouth, followed by the short, sharp, thick, slightly bitter taste of coffee.

Serves 6
scant $2/3$ cup superfine sugar
generous 1 cup water
$2^2/3$ cups strawberries
juice of $1/2$ lemon
half-and-half, to serve
(optional)

To make the sugar syrup, put the sugar and water into a pan over medium heat to dissolve the sugar. Bring to a boil, turn down the heat, and simmer for a couple of minutes. Remove from the heat and set aside until the sugar syrup has cooled.

Hull the strawberries and purée in a blender or food processor with the lemon juice. Pass through a strainer into a bowl. When the sugar syrup is completely cool, combine with the strawberry purée.

Pour the mixture into a shallow freezerproof container and place in the freezer for about 2 hours, until partially frozen.

Remove from the freezer and stir up the mixture with a fork, dragging in the frozen granita from the sides. Don't beat it as you would a sorbet—the texture of a granita is not the same, it is meant to be icy and crunchy. Return to the freezer until set.

To serve, pour a little half-and-half into each serving glass if you are feeling really decadent. Scoop the granita into the glasses and serve at once.

Fall

There is a certain, stirring excitement that comes with the change of every season. As ingredients begin to make their yearly reappearance, like old friends, the thrill for me is indescribable. It's a chance to revisit favorite recipes or try something new. Fall doesn't disappoint. There are quinces; wild mushrooms; walnuts; apples; hazelnuts; game; oily fish such as mackerel, sardines, and anchovies; mussels; pumpkins; black cabbage; puntarelle; and all those beautifully colored chards. Like the other seasons, if you choose to pay attention to it, fall has an extraordinary beauty all of its own.

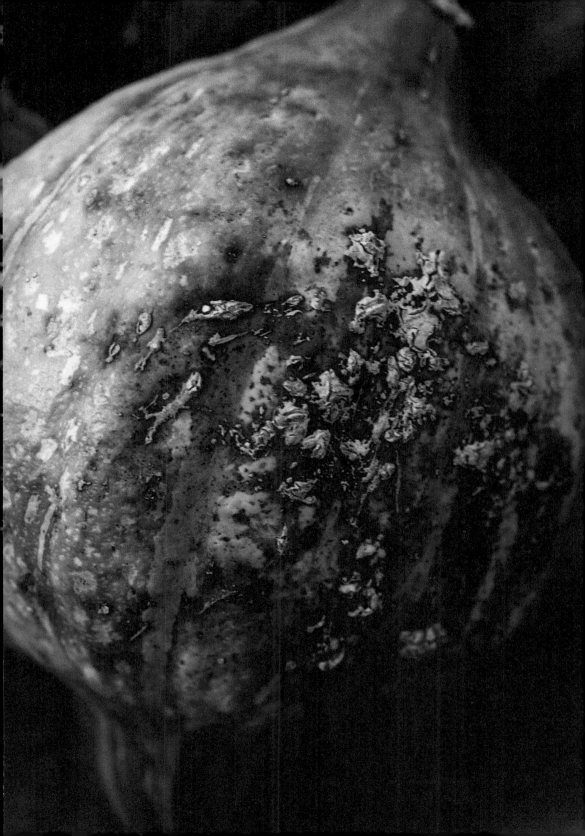

Cauliflower soup with Gorgonzola and pickled pear relish

This is one of my favorite fall soups. It is a perfect example of agrodolce, where a sweet, yet sharp relish balances out the deep flavor of the Gorgonzola so it doesn't become overwhelming. For me, it's the perfect lunch, with some textured chewy bread and a simple frisée salad dressed with walnut oil on the side.

Serves 4

1 medium cauliflower

1 tbsp unsalted butter

2 smallish yellow onions, peeled and finely sliced

4 thyme sprigs

2 bay leaves

sea salt and freshly ground black pepper

4 cups Chicken Stock (toolbox, page 18)

9 ounces Gorgonzola

1/3 cup crème fraîche

To serve

Pickled Pear Relish (toolbox, page 33)

minced curly parsley

Remove the outer leaves from the cauliflower and break it into small florets (don't bother to remove the stalk—it only adds to the flavor). Melt the butter gently in a pan (large enough to hold all your ingredients) over medium heat. Add the onions and sweat gently for 5 minutes, or until translucent.

Add the cauliflower, thyme, and bay leaves. Season with a little salt and pepper, to allow the flavors to adjust and find their feet. Pour in the stock, stir, and bring to a simmer. Then cover and simmer for 20 minutes, or until the cauliflower is very soft.

Crumble in the Gorgonzola and stir over low heat until it has melted into the soup. Add the crème fraîche and stir to combine.

Pick out the bay leaves and thyme sprigs, then tip the soup into a blender and whiz until really smooth. This will take a good minute or so, as often one or two little florets escape the blade.

Return the soup to the pan and reheat gently. Taste and add a little more salt and pepper if you think it needs it.

Ladle into warm soup plates and spoon a little pear relish into the center. Grind a little pepper over the soup, sprinkle with minced parsley, and serve.

Sweet potato and ginger soup

I am very partial to sweet potatoes. In Australia, we eat a lot of pumpkin, squash, and sweet potato and these vegetables remind me of home.

Serves 6

2 large sweet potatoes

2 tbsp unsalted butter

2 red onions, peeled and finely sliced

sea salt and freshly ground black pepper

1 tbsp grated fresh gingerroot

6¹/2 cups Chicken Stock (toolbox, page 18), or water if you prefer

²/3 cup heavy cream

1 tbsp tamari or soy sauce, or more to taste

1 tbsp maple syrup

juice of ¹/2 lime, or to taste

Peel and roughly chop the sweet potatoes. Melt the butter in a large pan over low heat. Add the onions, along with a pinch of salt, and sweat gently for 5 minutes, or until soft and translucent. Add the ginger, stir, then add the sweet potatoes and stir once more.

Pour in the chicken stock and bring to a boil. Immediately reduce the heat to a simmer and cook gently for 25 minutes, or until the sweet potatoes fall apart when prodded with a fork.

Remove from the heat and purée the soup in batches in a blender or food processor (don't fill it more than half full, otherwise the hot liquid might spill out of the top). Strain the soup through a fine strainer back into the pan and reheat gently.

Stir in the cream, tamari, and maple syrup, then squeeze in the lime juice. Check for seasoning and flavor—the soup should taste deep, warm, sweet, and slightly spicy. If the flavor seems slightly on the surface, just add a little more tamari—it will have a wonderful grounding effect. Serve warm.

Celery root rémoulade

I first ate this dish in Paris at the age of nineteen, soon after arriving to further my education. I had been cooking for only a short time and I was at that naive stage of thinking my cooking was about to change the world. I had combinations up my sleeve that no one had seen before … I now realize for good reason. This dish was the first of many lessons I learned about the beauty, simplicity, and elegance of classic French combinations. I often serve it with prosciutto, adding a scattering of toasted Périgord walnuts in fall, or a tiny drizzle of Basil Oil (toolbox, page 42) in the spring.

Serves 4

1 medium celery root

Dressing

generous 3/4 cup crème fraîche

1 1/2 tbsp coarse-grain mustard

finely grated zest and juice of 1/2 lemon

sea salt and freshly ground black pepper

To serve

12 wafer-thin slices of prosciutto

handful of curly parsley, minced

extra virgin olive oil, to drizzle

handful of walnuts, lightly toasted

First, make the dressing. In a bowl, mix together the crème fraîche, mustard, and lemon zest and juice. Season well with salt and pepper and set aside while you prepare the celery root.

Slice off either end of the celery root so it sits firmly on a cutting board, then peel away the skin with a sharp knife, following the contours of the vegetable. Split the celery root in half lengthwise, lay each half flat, and slice very finely into half-moon slices. Pile a few of these on top of each other and slice into very fine sticks (or julienne). Add to the dressing and repeat to cut up the rest of the slices.

Toss the celery root julienne in the dressing to coat well and check the seasoning. Spoon onto individual plates and drape the prosciutto slices on top. Sprinkle with minced parsley, drizzle with a little olive oil, and scatter over the walnuts to serve.

When I serve dishes cold,

like other chefs, I am referring to food served at room temperature. Anything eaten straight from the refrigerator doesn't have a chance of displaying any subtlety of flavor.

Wild mushrooms are among fall's bounty of treasures. Chanterelles, trumpets, honey fungus, porcini, and my favorite ovoli (Kaiser) are all in season. Shaved raw ovoli mushroom with wafer-thin slices of Parmesan and extra virgin olive oil is something everyone should try ... at least once.

Newly picked mushrooms have an earthy, pungent, meaty flavor when cooked that is rich and deeply satisfying. Each variety has a texture and taste all of its own ... it is really up to you to discover your favorites.

I prefer to do as little as possible to wild mushrooms. Fussy, complicated recipes only serve to mask their complex and particular flavor. In this case, less is definitely more.

Jerusalem artichokes, porcini, and Parmesan hats

This is an adaptation of a dish we prepared at the restaurant for a mushroom event, featuring shavings of rare and expensive ovoli mushrooms and Parmesan—a classic from the south of Italy. This recipe has a similar feel, celebrates the season in the same way, and yet has its very own distinctive quality. I am quite proud of its beauty and simplicity. It only works well as a light first course—it's almost like eating air!

Serves 6

6 ounces Parmesan

7 ounces fresh porcini mushrooms

2 tbsp extra virgin olive oil

finely grated zest and juice of 1 lemon

sea salt and freshly ground black pepper

1 pound 2 ounces Jerusalem artichokes (sunchokes), scrubbed

1 tbsp minced curly parsley

about 1 tbsp walnut oil, to drizzle

First, make the Parmesan hats—these are incredibly easy. Preheat the oven to 375°F (convection oven to 350°F). Line a baking sheet with waxed paper. Grate the Parmesan on a medium to fine grater and shape into 6 flat circular disks on the baking sheet. Place in the oven until melted and lightly golden, 4 to 6 minutes. Set aside to cool—the hats will firm up as they do so. (They can be kept in an airtight container between sheets of parchment paper for up to a week.)

Gently wipe the porcini with a clean, damp cloth. Using a mandoline, shave the mushrooms lengthwise as finely as possible. (If you do not have a mandoline, you should be able to achieve the same effect with a very sharp knife.) Place the porcini shavings in a bowl and toss with 1 tbsp of the olive oil, a third of the lemon zest, and a generous squeeze or two of lemon juice. Season with a little salt and pepper and set aside.

Shave the Jerusalem artichokes lengthwise very finely. Place in a separate bowl and dress in the same way as the mushrooms, with the remaining olive oil, lemon zest, juice, and seasoning.

Layer the Jerusalem artichoke and porcini shavings on individual plates or in shallow bowls, alternating the slices. Put the Parmesan hats on top and sprinkle with the minced parsley. Drizzle a little walnut oil around each plate and serve immediately.

I don't peel Jerusalem artichokes, because I love the contrast of their milky white center and nutty brown skin. Just wash them well (or scrub the skins if they are very dirty) and pat dry with a cloth.

Mushrooms always have a much better texture and flavor if you leave them alone during cooking as much as possible—a quick toss or two halfway through is plenty. Too much stirring and they are inclined to stew, resulting in a watery texture.

Chanterelles with fried egg and sourdough bread crumbs

I use mushrooms as often as I possibly can from late September through to mid-December. I adore their pungent earthy flavor and meaty texture. Quick, hot cooking, with as little adornment as possible, works best for me. Here, I serve them simply with fried eggs and the contrasting crunch of toasted bread crumbs. Fall salad greens—dressed with a vinaigrette of red wine vinegar and walnut oil—are the perfect complement.

Serves 2

1 pound 2 ounces fresh chanterelles

4 tbsp unsalted butter

sea salt and freshly ground black pepper

2 organic eggs

2 tbsp extra virgin olive oil

3 tbsp Sourdough Bread Crumbs (toolbox, page 24)

few fresh thyme or roughly chopped rosemary leaves

1 clove garlic, peeled and minced

lemon juice

1 tbsp minced curly parsley

1 tsp red wine vinegar or sherry vinegar

grated zest of 1 lemon, or to taste

Pick over the chanterelles with your fingers, removing any bits of grass, then wipe gently with a clean, damp cloth. Place a heavy skillet over medium heat. Add the butter and heat until melted and foaming, then add the mushrooms and season generously with salt and pepper. Increase the heat a little and leave the mushrooms to cook for 3 to 4 minutes, until tender, tossing them just once or twice during cooking.

Meanwhile, cook the eggs. Place a small nonstick skillet over medium heat. Add the olive oil and heat until it just starts to smoke. Crack the eggs into the pan and cook to your preference (I like a firm white with a soft yolk center). Scatter over the bread crumbs and thyme and allow them to just warm through.

When the mushrooms are ready, add the garlic, a squeeze of lemon juice, and half of the minced parsley. Pile onto two warm plates and slide the eggs and bread crumbs on top. Add the vinegar to the warm mushroom pan, stirring to deglaze, then pour over the eggs. Sprinkle with the lemon zest and the remaining parsley and serve at once, while piping hot!

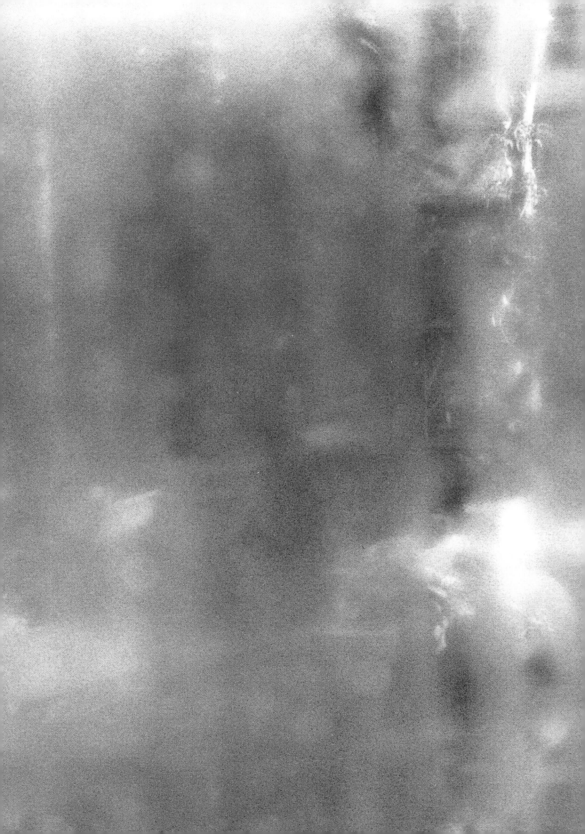

As an accompaniment, this warm salad works beautifully with roast lamb or broiled white fish, or you can simply serve it on its own with some good bread.

Warm broccoli salad with chile and garlic oil

The fibrous, leafy, sprouting broccoli that appears in the spring and fall is one of my favorite vegetables. Cook it correctly in heavily salted water and its inky green color is a sight to behold. Here it works brilliantly with the strong, bold flavors of anchovy and chile. Broccolini works equally well in this recipe. Take the time to infuse your own oil—it will have a flavor far superior to any store-bought alternative.

Serves 4 to 6

2 1/4 pounds sprouting broccoli or broccolini

sea salt and freshly ground black pepper

1 head of treviso or other radicchio

good handful of dandelion leaves or frisée

5 good-quality canned salted anchovy fillets, chopped

finely grated zest and juice of 1 lemon

1/2 cup Roasted Red Onions (toolbox, page 29)

1 tbsp little black olives (ideally, Niçoise or Ligurian)

Chile and garlic oil

2 cloves garlic, peeled

1 fresh red chile, halved and seeded

scant 1/3 cup extra virgin olive oil

Put a large pan of well-salted water on to boil (for the broccoli).

In the meantime, prepare the oil. Chop the garlic and chile as finely as you can. Place both in a bowl, pour on the olive oil, and let infuse while you cook your broccoli.

Tidy up the broccoli by trimming the base of the stalks and removing any leaves that look tired. Plunge into the boiling water and cook for 2 minutes. The stems should still be very crunchy. In the meantime, separate the treviso leaves.

Drain the broccoli, place in a warm bowl, and spoon over the infused oil. Add the treviso and dandelion leaves and toss to mix.

Scatter over the anchovies, lemon zest, roasted red onions, olives, a little salt, and a grinding of pepper. Lastly, squeeze over the lemon juice. Serve at once, layered onto warm plates.

Roasted squash with roasted tomatoes, feta, and basil oil

Fall delivers an amazing array of squashes, pumpkins, and gourds. Last year, we had the most beautiful display at the nursery, thanks to Geoff Noakes, who let us have more than 60 varieties. Some were better to cook than others—the onion squash was one of my favorites. If you can't get hold of it, I suggest you use kabocha or butternut squash instead. The flavor of butternut squash is most reliable, but it will need to be peeled.

Serves 4

1 to 2 onion or kabocha squash, about 2 pounds in total

3 or 4 tbsp extra virgin olive oil, to drizzle

1 dried red chile

small bunch of marjoram, leaves only

sea salt and freshly ground black pepper

1 pound 2 ounces small plum or cherry tomatoes

6 ounces good-quality feta

2 or 3 tbsp Roasted Red Onions (toolbox, page 29)

2 tbsp Basil Oil (toolbox, page 42)

Preheat the oven to 375°F (convection oven to 350°F). Using a sharp knife, cut each squash into 4 wedges and scrape out the seeds with a spoon. Lay the squash wedges, flesh side up, on a baking sheet and drizzle with olive oil. Crumble over the dried chile and scatter over the marjoram leaves. Season with a generous pinch of salt. Roast in the oven, until the squash is soft and slightly caramelized around the edges, 30 to 35 minutes.

About halfway through cooking, place the tomatoes on another baking sheet. Drizzle with a little olive oil and season with salt and pepper. Roast in the oven, alongside the squash, for 15 minutes. Let the squash and tomatoes cool to room temperature. Meanwhile, cut the feta into thin slices.

To assemble, pile the roasted squash wedges and tomatoes onto individual plates or in shallow bowls and scatter over the roasted red onions. Arrange the feta on top and/or next to the squash, then spoon over the basil oil and a little more olive oil. Now you are ready to serve!

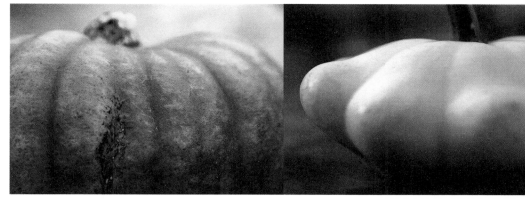

Spiced eggplant and sweet potato curry with spinach

This is a lovely fragrant curry. The sweet potato and eggplant absorb all the beautiful complex flavors that are laid down at the start of the dish. I particularly like to eat it with a simple flatbread, but it's also good with boiled rice. A cucumber salad with mint and cilantro—dressed with lime juice, fish sauce, and sesame oil—is an ideal side dish.

Serves 4

1 pound 2 ounces eggplants, trimmed

sea salt

1 pound 2 ounces sweet potatoes

2 lemongrass stalks

2 tbsp chopped cilantro stems

5 cloves garlic, peeled

2-inch piece fresh gingerroot, peeled

1 large fresh red chile, stalk removed

6 lime leaves

4 tbsp vegetable oil

3 red onions, peeled and sliced

1 tbsp Roasted Spice Mix (toolbox, page 16)

2 cups canned coconut milk

2 tbsp tamarind water (see page 205)

3 tbsp fish sauce

2 tbsp jaggery or superfine sugar

14 ounces young, tender spinach leaves, well washed

First prepare the eggplants. Cut them in half lengthwise and then into 1-inch cubes. Place in a colander, salt well, and set aside to degorge the bitter juices for 10 minutes. Peel the sweet potatoes and cut into 1-inch cubes.

Meanwhile, peel off the outer layer of the lemongrass, bruise the base with the back of a knife, then cut off and discard the top half (it is dry and unyielding). Put the lemongrass in a food processor along with the cilantro, garlic, ginger, chile, lime leaves, and 2 tbsp water. Blend for about a minute to a paste.

Pat the eggplant cubes dry with paper towels. Place a large, nonstick skillet over medium-high heat, add 3 tbsp of the oil, and heat until almost smoking. Cook the eggplant in small batches, until golden brown on all sides, then remove and drain on paper towels.

Place a large pan or cooking pot over medium heat and add the remaining 1 tbsp oil. When it is hot, add the onions and cook, stirring from time to time until translucent, about 5 minutes. Add the lemongrass paste together with the roasted spice mix and cook, stirring, for 3 to 4 minutes to release the flavors.

Pour in the coconut milk, then add the tamarind water, fish sauce, and sugar. Stir well and bring to a boil, then add the sweet potatoes. Turn down the heat and simmer for 10 minutes, then add the browned eggplant and cook for another 5 minutes.

In a separate pan, cook the spinach quickly in batches over medium-high heat, with just the water clinging to the leaves from washing, until just wilted. Tip into a strainer and refresh under cold running water, then squeeze dry between the palms of your hands.

Just before serving, add the spinach to the curry and gently warm through. Taste and adjust the seasoning and flavorings if necessary, perhaps adding a little more sugar or fish sauce. You are looking for a balance of sweet, sour, hot, and salty flavors.

Mussels with fennel, saffron, and spinach

Mussels are at their best during the fall. I miss them during the summer months when they are not available and begin to pester my fish supplier, Colin, for them early in September. Being a perfectionist, Colin will not sell me anything that is less than perfect ... last year he kept me waiting until almost the end of September, but that first batch of mussels was well worth the wait. Plump and deep coral in color, they are beautiful in this timeless combination. *Illustrated on previous page.*

Serves 4

2¹/4 pounds live mussels

3/4 cup dry white wine

2 large shallots, peeled and minced

4 bay leaves

few thyme sprigs

10 black peppercorns

1 medium fennel bulb

1 tbsp unsalted butter

2 tsp saffron threads

sea salt and freshly ground black pepper

generous 1 cup water

generous 1 cup crème fraîche

5 ounces young, tender spinach leaves, well washed

First, clean the mussels thoroughly. Remove the tenacious beards, then pull away any seaweed attached to the shells and wash the shells well under cold running water.

Pour the wine into a large heavy pan over low heat, add the shallots, bay leaves, thyme, and peppercorns and bring to a simmer. Tip the mussels into the pan, increase the heat slightly, and cover with a tight-fitting lid. Cook until the mussels open, by shaking the pan now and then to give the mussels room, for 4 to 5 minutes.

Meanwhile, prepare the fennel. Trim off the base and discard the fibrous outer layer, then slice finely.

Remove the lid from the pan and tip the mussels into a colander set over a bowl to catch the liquid. Wipe out the pan and return to low heat. Add the butter and once it has melted, put in the fennel slices, saffron, and a little salt and pepper (remembering that the mussels may be quite salty). Sweat gently for about 10 minutes, until the fennel is soft.

Meanwhile, discard any unopened mussels. Strain the mussel cooking liquor and add it to the fennel with the water and crème fraîche. Stir well and bring to a boil. Simmer for 1 to 2 minutes, then add the spinach and mussels. Cook for another minute to wilt the spinach and warm the mussels through. Check the seasoning.

Ladle into warm bowls and serve with crusty open-textured white bread and beautiful unsalted butter.

Griddled scallops with radicchio, sourdough bread crumbs, and anchovy dressing

This salad is full of texture and has a wonderful, intense flavor. The sweet plump scallops work beautifully with it—just make sure you cook them as quickly as possible, so they remain succulent. Allow 4 to 6 scallops per person, according to size, and ask your fish supplier to shell and clean them for you. You may need to cook the scallops in two batches, depending on the number and your pan.

Serves 4

16 to 24 sea scallops

2 small heads of radicchio

4 tbsp Sourdough Bread Crumbs (toolbox, page 24)

2 organic eggs, hard-cooked, peeled, and grated

1 tbsp minced curly parsley

juice of 1/2 small lemon, or to taste

1/4 cup extra virgin olive oil

olive oil, for cooking

sea salt and freshly ground black pepper

Anchovy vinaigrette

6 fine-quality canned anchovy fillets in olive oil, drained

1 shallot, peeled and chopped

1 1/2 tbsp good-quality red wine vinegar

freshly ground black pepper

generous 1/3 cup extra virgin olive oil

To finish

finely grated zest of 1 lemon

Trim away the tough muscle from the side of each scallop, then set aside at room temperature while you prepare the salad. Remove any discolored outer leaves from the radicchio, then cut in half and slice finely (as if you were making a coleslaw). Place in a bowl and add the sourdough bread crumbs, eggs, and parsley.

Now, make the anchovy vinaigrette. Put the anchovies in a blender with the shallot, vinegar, and a generous grinding of pepper. With the motor running, slowly pour in the olive oil, to create an emulsified sauce. (Don't panic if the sauce splits, though; it will still taste delicious.)

Squeeze the lemon juice over the radicchio, drizzle over the extra virgin olive oil, and toss lightly with your fingers (easily the best implements for tossing salads). Place a pile of salad on each plate.

Heat a heavy skillet or griddle over medium heat, then add a good splash of olive oil. Season the scallops well with salt and pepper and, when the pan is smoking, add them to the skillet one by one. (Take care, as they may well splutter because of their high water content.) Cook for 1 minute, then turn and cook for a minute on the other side. The scallops should have a golden crust on both sides and feel springy when you press them gently.

Lay the scallops on top of the dressed radicchio. Spoon over the anchovy vinaigrette and scatter with lemon zest. Serve immediately, while the scallops are piping hot.

Roasted halibut with Sichuan eggplants

The flavor of these eggplants is based on the style of cooking found in the province of Sichuan in China. Said by some to be the greatest of all Chinese cooking styles, it certainly has a complexity about it that I love. If you can find them, fiery Sichuan peppercorns—roasted and ground—give this dish its final hat. The pickled eggplants would also work brilliantly served cold with slices of rare roast beef or pink lamb.

Serves 4

4 halibut fillets, about 5¹/2 ounces each

sea salt and freshly ground black pepper

1¹/2 tbsp olive oil

Pickled eggplants

1 pound 2 ounces eggplants

sea salt

bunch of cilantro

3 tbsp vegetable oil

2-inch piece fresh gingerroot, peeled and minced

3 shallots, peeled and minced

4 cloves garlic, peeled and minced

2 tbsp light soy sauce

2 tbsp dark soy sauce

5 tbsp rice wine vinegar

5 tbsp Shaoxing wine (rice wine)

1 tbsp Chile Oil (toolbox, page 44)

4 tbsp superfine sugar

1 tsp Sichuan peppercorns, roasted and ground (optional)

To finish

extra virgin olive oil, to drizzle

First, prepare the eggplants. Cut them in half lengthwise and then into 1-inch cubes. Place in a colander, salt well, and set aside for 10 minutes. Meanwhile, separate the cilantro stems, saving a handful of the leaves. Pound the stems using a mortar and pestle. Pat the eggplant cubes dry with paper towels.

Place a wok over medium-high heat, add the vegetable oil and heat until almost smoking. Cook the eggplant cubes in small batches, until golden brown on all sides, then remove and drain on paper towels.

Pour off excess oil from the wok, then add the ginger, shallots, garlic, and pounded cilantro stems. Stir-fry for 1 to 2 minutes, then add the soy sauces, vinegar, wine, chile oil, and sugar. Let bubble vigorously for a minute or so.

Return the eggplant to the wok, turn down the heat a little, and cook for another 2 minutes, tossing and turning the eggplant so it absorbs the sweet, sour flavors. Roughly tear the cilantro leaves and toss them through the eggplant with the ground Sichuan pepper.

To cook the halibut, preheat the oven to 375°F (convection oven to 350°F). Season the fish generously with salt and pepper. Heat a large ovenproof pan that will hold the fish without overcrowding (use two pans if necessary). Add the olive oil and when it is just starting to smoke, lay the halibut, skin side down, in the pan. Cook for 2 minutes without moving or turning, then place the pan in the oven (still without turning the fish) and cook until the skin is gloriously brown and crunchy, 2 to 3 minutes.

Place a spoonful or two of the pickled eggplants on each warm plate. Carefully turn the fish and lay it skin side up alongside. Drizzle with extra virgin olive oil and serve.

Pan-fried sea bass with braised fennel and ginger

This is definitely one of my favorite fish dishes...the delicate taste and texture of sea bass work beautifully with the aniseedy flavor of fennel. Beurre blanc complements all white fish—you could substitute halibut, haddock, or cod here if you prefer.

Serves 4

4 sea bass fillets (with skin), about 6 ounces each

sea salt and freshly ground black pepper

1 to 2 tbsp olive oil

1 tbsp minced parsley (optional)

Braised fennel

6 fennel bulbs

generous 1 cup dry white wine

13/4 cups Chicken Stock (toolbox, page 18)

1-inch piece very fresh gingerroot, peeled and cut into thin stick slivers

1 tbsp fennel seeds, roasted and crushed

Beurre blanc

1 shallot, peeled and minced

8 black peppercorns

few thyme sprigs

4 tbsp dry white wine, such as Sauvignon Blanc

4 tbsp good-quality white wine vinegar

1 tbsp heavy cream

generous 1 cup unsalted butter, cut into 3/4-inch cubes and well chilled

sea salt and freshly ground white pepper

Preheat the oven to 375°F (convection oven to 350°F). First prepare the fennel. Trim and set aside any feathery fronds for garnish. Remove the fibrous outer layer, cut each bulb into quarters, and place in a shallow baking pan. Pour over the wine and stock, then sprinkle with the ginger and fennel seeds. Cover with foil and bake until the fennel is soft and almost falling apart, 35 to 45 minutes.

Meanwhile, make the beurre blanc. Put the shallots, peppercorns, thyme, wine, and vinegar into a small pan. Bring to a boil over medium heat and reduce until only 1 or 2 tbsp of liquid remains. Strain the liquid, discarding the flavorings and return to the pan. Reduce the heat to very low and add the cream, then gradually begin adding the butter, a couple of cubes at a time, whisking continuously to emulsify and taking care that the sauce does not boil. Continue until all the butter is used and you have a creamy, velvety sauce. Season with a little salt and white pepper.

Keep the beurre blanc warm at the back of the stove or in a bowl over a pan of warm water. (It is a delicate sauce and cannot be reheated, otherwise it will curdle.) Remove the fennel from the oven when it is cooked and keep warm. Leave the oven on.

To cook the fish, generously season the skin side only with salt and pepper. Heat the olive oil in a heavy ovenproof skillet (use two skillets if necessary to avoid overcrowding). When the oil is very hot, lay the fish gently in the pan and cook without turning until the skin is very crisp, about 4 minutes. Place the pan in the oven for 3 to 4 minutes to finish cooking.

To serve, spoon a little of the braised fennel into the center of each warm plate. Lay the fish fillets, skin side up, on top and spoon over the beurre blanc. Finish with a scattering of chopped fennel fronds or some minced parsley.

Pan-roasted guinea fowl with parsley sauce

Parsley sauce reminds me of a warm cotton blanket—cozy and snuggly, but still somehow fresh and clean. The trick is to use a lot of parsley—the sauce should be laden with vibrant green flecks. It goes equally well with poached ham or beef brisket, or you could serve it with poached wild salmon.

Serves 6

6 guinea fowl supremes (bone-in, skin-on breasts with the first wing joint attached)

sea salt and freshly ground black pepper

olive oil, for cooking

Parsley sauce

5 ounces curly parsley, stems removed, plus extra to serve

2 cups heavy cream

freshly grated nutmeg

1¹/₂ tsp finely grated lemon zest, or to taste

sea salt and freshly ground black pepper

First, make the parsley sauce. Put a pan of well-salted water on to boil (it should be as salty as the sea). Plunge the parsley leaves into the boiling water for 30 seconds. Remove and refresh in ice water (to keep your parsley a beautiful, bright color). Drain and set aside.

Pour the cream into a heavy pan and bring almost to a boil. Turn down the heat and let bubble to reduce by about a third, until it has thickened enough to coat the back of a wooden spoon. Add the blanched parsley leaves and boil for a moment longer. Remove from the heat and purée in a blender until you have a beautiful fine-textured sauce.

Add a generous grating of nutmeg and the lemon zest, then season well with salt and a good grinding of pepper. Your sauce is now ready; keep it warm.

Guinea fowl has a wonderful depth of flavor and a real warmth that is perfect for fall. An earthy purée of rutabaga, enriched with butter and seasoned with black pepper, is an excellent accompaniment.

Preheat the oven to 450°F (convection oven to 425°F). Season the guinea fowl generously with salt and pepper all over. Place a heavy ovenproof skillet over medium-high heat and heat until smoking. Pour in about 1 tbsp olive oil, then brown the guinea fowl in batches. Lay two supremes in the skillet, skin side down, and let color for 3 minutes—resist the temptation to play with them. Transfer to a baking sheet (without turning) and brown the rest of the supremes in the same way.

Finish cooking the guinea fowl in the oven until the skin is crisp and crunchy and the breast meat is succulent, moist, and cooked through, 6 to 8 minutes. Let rest in a warm place for 5 minutes.

Arrange the guinea fowl supremes on warm plates, on a bed of rutabaga purée if you like, and ladle the warm parsley sauce generously over the top. Scatter over chopped parsley and serve.

Slow-cooked veal with spinach, carrots, and lemon

I haven't particularly come across this dish anywhere before, but it has a sense of classicism about it. As I adore wet food—food you can drag your bread through—I find it very appealing. It works well with a celery root purée and blanched green beans, tossed with unsalted butter and a little minced garlic. Or you could serve it simply with a baguette and a salad of bitter fall greens.

Serves 6 to 8

4¹/2 pounds boned shoulder of veal

1 tbsp olive oil

sea salt and freshly ground black pepper

3 yellow onions, peeled and sliced

juice of 1 lemon

1¹/2 tbsp Dijon mustard

5 carrots, peeled and cut into big chunks

3 cloves garlic, peeled and minced

a few thyme sprigs

3 or 4 bay leaves

generous 6¹/3 cups veal or Chicken Stock (toolbox, page 18)

5 ounces young, tender spinach leaves, well washed

generous 3/4 cup crème fraîche

Slow-cooked dishes

work better if the pieces of meat are generous in size. They tend to shrink during cooking and, if you're not careful, you can end up with something resembling a school dinner. Food to me must always be identifiable.

Trim the veal of any fat and cut into big chunks, about 2¹/2 inches. Heat the olive oil in a Dutch oven or other heavy pot over medium heat. Season the meat all over with salt and pepper. When the oil is very hot, brown the veal, a few pieces at a time, turning them to color evenly. (It is important not to crowd the pot, otherwise the meat will stew.) Once the pieces are golden brown all over, remove from the pot and set aside on a plate while you brown the rest in batches.

Lower the heat slightly, add the onions to the Dutch oven, and cook for 4 to 5 minutes, until translucent. Squeeze over the lemon juice and stir well to deglaze. Add the mustard, carrots, garlic, thyme, and bay leaves. Sauté briefly, then pour in the stock and simmer for a few minutes. Return the meat to the pot and turn the heat down to very low. Put the lid on, then leave alone to cook for 45 minutes.

Meanwhile, place a large pan over medium heat and add the spinach with just the water clinging to the leaves after washing. (This will be sufficient to create steam to wilt the spinach.) Once the leaves have wilted, drain and refresh in cold water, then tip into a colander and drain well. Using your hands, squeeze out as much excess water as possible and set the spinach aside until needed.

After 45 minutes, the veal should be tender and the stock will have a rich, warming taste. Discard the herbs, then add the crème fraîche and increase the heat a little—to enable the sauce to slowly reduce and thicken. This will take 10 minutes or so. Taste and adjust the seasoning—you'll probably need a generous grinding of pepper and a good pinch of salt. Add the spinach, stir through, and serve.

Lamb with broccoli, anchovy, and harissa

This dish is strong, honest, and punchy and its colors work beautifully on a plate. Surprisingly, perhaps, anchovies are brilliant with both lamb and broccoli. Harissa is a hot, spicy Moroccan paste, traditionally made with dried chiles. I prefer a gentler version, so I make it with fresh chiles and red bell peppers—the taste is smoother and warmer. You can, of course, add more chiles if you wish. Ask your butcher to butterfly (bone out) the lamb for you.

Serves 6 to 8

1 leg of lamb, butterflied, about 4¹/2 pounds

5 anchovy fillets in oil, drained and cut in half

2 or 3 cloves garlic, peeled and cut into slivers

8 tbsp unsalted butter, softened

sea salt and freshly ground black pepper

Harissa

2 tbsp Roasted Spice Mix (toolbox, page 16)

2 red bell peppers, peeled, cored, and seeded

4 cloves garlic, peeled

pinch of sea salt

5¹/2 tbsp extra virgin olive oil

5 fresh red chiles, thinly sliced

bunch of cilantro, roughly chopped

1 tsp fish sauce

2 tbsp jaggery or superfine sugar

lemon juice

Broccoli

1¹/2 pounds sprouting broccoli or broccolini

1¹/2 tbsp extra virgin olive oil

finely grated zest of 1 lemon

sea salt and freshly ground black pepper

First, make the harissa. Put all the ingredients, except the lemon juice, into a blender or food processor and blitz until smooth. Tip into a bowl, stir in a couple of drops of lemon juice, and set aside until ready to use.

Preheat the oven to 375°F (convection oven to 350°F). Lay the lamb flat, skin side up, on a cutting board and make about 10 small incisions, ¹/2 inch deep, all over the surface using a paring knife. Poke one anchovy fillet half and insert 1 or 2 garlic slivers into each little pocket. Smear the butter all over the skin, using your fingers, then season the lamb liberally with pepper and sparingly with salt. Place in a shallow roasting pan, cover with foil, and roast in the oven for 20 minutes.

Remove the foil and return the lamb to the oven to crisp and brown the skin, 15 to 20 minutes. Because it is butterflied, the meat cooks far more quickly than it would on the bone. It should be pink inside, but not rare. (I much prefer the taste of pink lamb.) Cover loosely with foil and set aside in a warm place to rest for 20 minutes. Save the pan juices.

Meanwhile, prepare the broccoli. Trim off the base of the stalks and remove any bruised or damaged leaves. Plunge into a pan of well-salted boiling water, return to a boil, and cook for 2 minutes. Drain and immediately dress with the olive oil and lemon zest. Season with a little salt and pepper.

To assemble, carve the lamb into thin slices (or thicker ones if you prefer). Place 2 or 3 slices on each plate and spoon over the pan juices. Lay the broccoli on top of the lamb and spoon over the harissa. Serve at once.

Lamb with prunes, chile, cilantro, and spice mix

I really love the process of long, slow cooking—how with time, thought, and patience, a dish transforms itself from simple ingredients to complex layered flavors that enliven the palate and satisfy the soul. This dish, more than any other, typifies the way I cook. Layering flavors on top of each other, countering the warmth of spices with the cool of lime, balancing salty and sweet flavors. Base notes resonate with top notes to create a harmony that feels just right to me.

Serves 6

1 boned medium leg of lamb, about 3¼ pounds

sea salt and freshly ground black pepper

1 tbsp olive oil

generous bunch of cilantro

3 red onions, peeled and finely sliced

1-inch piece very fresh gingerroot, peeled and minced

1 tbsp tamarind water (see page 205)

3 cloves garlic, peeled and chopped

2 fresh red chiles, minced (seeds retained)

2 tbsp Roasted Spice Mix (toolbox, page 16)

6½ cups Chicken Stock (toolbox, page 18)

2 (14-ounce) cans good-quality chopped tomatoes

3 or 4 bay leaves

2 cinnamon sticks

generous ⅓ cup tamari or soy sauce, or to taste

5 tbsp maple syrup, or to taste

1 cup prunes

juice of 1 or 2 limes, to taste

Cut the lamb into 2-inch pieces, trimming away any fat. Season the meat generously with salt and pepper. Place a large heavy pan over medium heat and add the olive oil. When it is very hot (starting to smoke), brown the lamb in small batches (to avoid overcrowding the pan). Turn the meat to color on all sides, but don't fiddle with it any more than you need to. As each piece is ready, remove it from the pan and set aside on a plate, while you brown the rest. Wash the cilantro, separate the leaves and set aside for garnishing if you like, then mince the stems.

Once all the meat is browned and put aside, pour off excess fat from the pan, lower the heat slightly, and add the onions. Cook, stirring, for 5 minutes, or until they have begun to soften. Add the ginger, tamarind water, garlic, chiles, spice mix, and chopped cilantro. Cook, stirring, for another 5 minutes. Add the stock, increase the heat a little, and bring to a boil. Add the tomatoes, bay leaves, and cinnamon and bring back to a boil.

Put the meat back into the pan, cover with the lid, and turn down the heat to low. Cook, stirring occasionally, for 45 minutes. After this time, the meat should be almost tender and your base note flavors in place. To balance the flavors, you now need to add the tamari (for salt, depth, and color), maple syrup (for sweetness), prunes (for texture), and lime juice to balance the earthy tones of the spices. Stir well, turn up the heat very slightly, and cook for another 30 minutes.

Before serving, check the seasoning and scatter over some roughly torn cilantro leaves if you like.

I like to serve this with a sweet potato purée (see page 182) rather than couscous, and a peppery green salad dressed with grated Parmesan, lemon zest, olive oil, and lemon juice. A cooling dollop of yogurt flavored with a hint of chile, cilantro, lime, and olive oil also goes well.

Sweet potato purée with tamari, maple syrup, and chile

This is a punchy, sweet-tasting purée, which works particularly well with Middle Eastern–flavored dishes.

Serves 4

2 large sweet potatoes, peeled

1 small fresh red chile, halved (seeds retained)

sea salt and freshly ground black pepper

small bunch of cilantro

4 tbsp unsalted butter

1 tbsp extra virgin olive oil

2 tbsp tamari or soy sauce

2 tbsp maple syrup

Cut the sweet potatoes into rough chunks, then place in a pan and add the chile with its seeds. Pour in enough cold water to cover, add a good pinch of salt, and bring to a boil over medium heat. Lower the heat and simmer for about 15 minutes, until the sweet potato is very tender and falling apart. Drain in a colander.

Tip the sweet potatoes and chile into a blender. Add the cilantro leaves and stems, butter, olive oil, tamari, and maple syrup and purée until very smooth. Taste and adjust the seasoning. The purée should have a deep, sweet, hot, velvety taste.

If necessary, return to the pan and reheat gently, stirring, to serve.

As a rule of thumb, all vegetables that grow below the ground go into cold water and all vegetables that grow above ground go into boiling water.

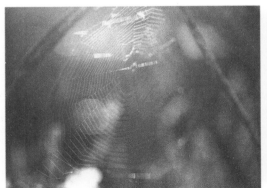

Cavolo nero with garlic and Parmesan

First grown in Italy, this beautiful, ruffled, inky black member of the cabbage family was almost impossible to find outside of Tuscany until a few years ago. Thanks to the work of Ruth Rogers and Rose Gray, it is now more widely available and I love to cook with it. As an accompaniment, this is beautiful with roast lamb, or you can simply serve it as a stand-alone dish—delicious on bruschetta.

Serves 4 to 6

2¼ pounds cavolo nero (black cabbage or dinosaur kale)

sea salt and freshly ground black pepper

7 tbsp unsalted butter

1 tbsp extra virgin olive oil

1 red onion, peeled and minced

3 cloves garlic, peeled and minced

5 ounces Parmesan, freshly grated

Wash the cavolo nero in cold water, then drain and cut out the tough white center, leaving just the crinkly leaves.

Bring a large pan of well-salted water to a boil, add the cavolo nero, and cook for 2 minutes after the water has returned to a boil. Drain and refresh under cold running water. Drain well.

In a separate pan, melt the butter with the olive oil and add the onion, garlic, a generous pinch of salt, and a good grinding of pepper. Sweat gently for about 10 minutes, until the onion is soft and translucent.

Add the cabbage and toss well to coat all the leaves in the garlicky butter. When the cavolo nero is warmed through, add the Parmesan, toss well, and serve.

Fall coleslaw

This strong, crunchy, earthbound coleslaw comprises everything that is good about fall—apples, cobnuts, red cabbage, and beets. My last meal on Earth would have to be some sort of salad ... this might just be it! Pretty pink and white candy striped beets look amazing, but the purple or golden variety will taste just as good. Pomegranate molasses adds an extra dimension to the flavor if you can find it.

Serves 4

1 cup shelled cobnuts or hazelnuts, very roughly chopped

1 pomegranate, quartered

1/4 red cabbage, cored

1 fennel bulb

4 beets, washed

3 carrots, peeled

4 crisp apples (such as Gala or Jonagold)

small bunch of tarragon, leaves only, minced

sea salt and freshly ground black pepper

1 tbsp extra virgin olive oil

juice of 1/2 lemon, or to taste

Dressing

2 organic egg yolks

1 tbsp honey

1 1/2 tsp Dijon mustard

1 tbsp cream

1 tbsp cider vinegar

1 tsp pomegranate molasses (optional)

sea salt and freshly ground black pepper

3/4 cup mild olive oil

To finish

finely chopped parsley

Preheat the oven to 375°F (convection oven to 350°F). Spread the cobnuts on a baking sheet and gently toast them in the oven for 3 to 4 minutes, just to release their flavor. Set aside to cool.

Carefully extract the seeds from the pomegranate, avoiding the bitter membrane; set aside.

Finely slice the cabbage into thin ribbons. Cut off the base of the fennel bulb and remove the tough outer layer, then slice very finely. Cut the beets into very thin circles. Shave the carrots into long ribbons, using a swivel vegetable peeler. Quarter and core the apples, leaving the skin on, then slice thinly.

Place the cabbage, fennel, beets, carrots, apples, and tarragon in a bowl and season with the salt and pepper. Drizzle over the olive oil and squeeze over the lemon juice. Toss together gently with your hands and set aside while you make the dressing.

For the dressing, put the egg yolks into a bowl. Add the honey, mustard, cream, vinegar, and molasses and whisk together to combine. Season with a little salt and pepper, then pour in the olive oil in a slow stream, whisking as you do so to emulsify. It should have the consistency of a very loose mayonnaise.

Divide the salad among individual plates, piling it high. Drizzle over the dressing, sprinkle with chopped parsley, and scatter the cobnuts and pomegranate seeds around the plate to serve.

Baked quince with honey, bay, and verjuice

Of all the fruits this season offers, I am most excited at the arrival of the first pale green quinces in early fall. I love the look of our little gnarled tree laden with pear-shaped fruit. The way that long, slow cooking transforms quinces into sweet, burnt amber jewels is a constant source of amazement to me.

Serves 4

4 quinces

generous ⅓ cup verjuice

4 tbsp good honey
(preferably, locally sourced)

2 cinnamon sticks

1 vanilla bean, split in half
lengthwise

finely pared zest of 1 lemon

4 bay leaves

strained plain yogurt, to serve

Preheat the oven to 325°F (convection oven to 300°F). Wipe the quinces clean, removing the furry layer with a dry cloth. Quarter them lengthwise, but don't bother to remove the seeds or core.

Place the quince quarters, cut side up, in a baking sheet and pour over the verjuice. Drizzle with the honey and scatter over the cinnamon sticks, vanilla bean, lemon zest, and bay leaves.

Cover very lightly with foil and bake for about 2½ hours, turning the fruit halfway through cooking. The quinces are ready when they are soft, sticky, and a beautiful burnt orange color. Discard the cinnamon sticks, vanilla bean, and bay leaves. Serve warm or at room temperature, with strained plain yogurt.

Verjuice is made from the juice of unripe grapes. It is slightly tart and adds a little acidity without overpowering the flavors in this dish. If you can't find verjuice, use apple juice instead for this recipe and add a squeeze of lemon juice.

Baked blackberry and ginger pudding

I generally prefer clean, light, fresh fruit-based desserts that don't sit heavily at the end of a meal. But as the weather turns cooler and the days become shorter, there is something undeniably comforting about this warm, sweet pudding and the slightly spicy aroma that emerges when you plunge your spoon in. Pair it with a beautiful, thick unpasteurized cream and you have a really lovely fall dessert.

Serves 4

7 tbsp unsalted butter, softened, plus extra to grease

1/2 cup superfine sugar

2 organic eggs

scant 3/4 cup self-rising flour

finely grated zest of 2 lemons

4 pieces of preserved ginger in syrup, drained and minced

sea salt

2 tbsp corn syrup

2 tbsp honey

12 plump blackberries

thick cream, to serve

Preheat the oven to 375°F (convection oven to 350°F). Butter 4 individual ovenproof ramekins or custard cups, 2/3-cup capacity, and set aside. In a large bowl, cream together the softened butter and sugar until pale and smooth. Add the eggs, one at a time, beating well after each addition. Sift in the flour from a good height and fold in gently. Finally, add the lemon zest, preserved ginger, and a restrained pinch of salt. Fold in until evenly mixed.

Mix together the corn syrup and honey and spoon 1 tbsp into each mold. Add 3 blackberries to each and then spoon the pudding on top. Cover each mold loosely with a piece of buttered foil and place the molds on a baking sheet. Bake, until well risen and cooked through, 25 to 30 minutes. To test, stick a skewer into the center; it should come out clean.

Run a knife around each pudding and turn out onto a warm plate. Serve with a pitcher of cream.

Apple and eau-de-vie snow

In early October, we get deliveries of rare breed English apples as the country celebrates National Apple Week. We have a set of very old scales on a rickety old table outside the Cafe and sell them by the pound. The apples are never around for long, as people find their fall beauty hard to resist. I take this opportunity to cook with apples as often as possible, and this is one of the desserts I love to make. It's not really snow at all—we stole the name because it is vaguely based on the principle.

Serves 6

1¹/4 cups superfine sugar

2 cups water

1 vanilla bean, split lengthwise

6 crisp, sweet apples (such as Gala)

ground cinnamon

8 organic egg whites

sea salt

2 tbsp apple eau-de-vie or apple brandy

First, make the sugar syrup. Put the sugar, water, and vanilla bean into a heavy pan over low heat and stir a couple of times. Once the sugar has dissolved, turn up the heat a little to bring the liquid to a simmer.

In the meantime, peel, core, and chop the apples, quite roughly. Add to the sugar syrup and cook for 5 to 6 minutes, until tender but still holding their shape. Remove from the heat and let the apple pieces cool in the liquid. (This allows the sugary vanilla flavor to infuse them.)

Once cooled, remove the apples with a slotted spoon and put them into a food processor or blender with 2 tbsp of the sugar syrup and a pinch of cinnamon. Whiz to a very pale, smooth purée. Set aside.

Whisk the egg whites in a clean bowl with a pinch of salt to firm peaks. Add to the apple purée and whisk lightly to combine.

Pour the mixture into an ice-cream maker and churn according to your manufacturer's instructions, until the ice cream has just begun to set. Add the alcohol and continue to churn until you have a soft, feathery, light slush. Scoop into glasses and serve at once.

This "snow" is cold and pure in feel. As you eat it, the coolness is refreshing, yet the intense flavor of the apple eau-de-vie almost warms you at the same time—like a fire in your chest.

Walnut and honey tart

I think this tart originates from Provence, but I can't be absolutely sure. It is one of my favorites and a lovely way to enjoy fresh walnuts during their short season.

Serves 8 to 10

9 ounces Pie Dough (toolbox, page 242, 1/2 recipe)

flour, to dust

4 cups shelled walnut halves (preferably, freshly shelled)

1 tbsp walnut oil

1 1/4 cups superfine sugar

1/2 cup water

6 tbsp thick honey

4 tbsp crème fraîche, plus extra to serve

Roll out the pie dough on a lightly floured counter to a large circle, about 1/8 inch thick. Using your rolling pin, carefully lift the dough and drape it over a 10-inch tart pan, about 1 inch deep, with a removable bottom. Press the dough into the edges and side of the pan, using your fingers. Trim excess dough away from the rim, so that your tart shell looks neat and prick the base here and there with a fork. Refrigerate for 20 minutes.

Meanwhile, preheat the oven to 375°F (convection oven to 350°F). Place the walnuts on a baking sheet, drizzle over the walnut oil, and toss gently with your hands to coat them in the oil (being careful not to break them up too much). Toast in the oven for 2 to 3 minutes only, to intensify their flavor. Set aside while you make the caramel. Leave the oven on.

Put the sugar and water in a heavy pan over medium heat to dissolve the sugar, then increase the heat and allow the sugar syrup to bubble, until caramelized to a pale amber color. Immediately tip in the walnuts and stir to coat well. Remove from the heat and add the honey and crème fraîche. Mix well with a wooden spoon and let cool.

Line the pastry shell with waxed paper and dried beans and bake "blind" for 15 minutes. Remove the beans and paper and return to the oven until the pastry base is golden brown, about 5 minutes. Remove from the oven and let cool.

Spread the walnut filling in the pastry shell, piling it high so that it looks generous and beautiful. Serve with crème fraîche.

Winter

*With its long hours of darkness and a sky that
seems to sit so low that it rests on my shoulders, the
English winter can seem very bleak to me. It can also
feel a little desolate in terms of fruit and vegetables.
Once the abundance of fall has dwindled, we are left
with apples, pears, chards, and root vegetables,
but little else. Fortunately, Italy brings us wonderful
bitter winter greens. Blood oranges, too, are in season.
At their best, these have a superb, clean flavor—the
perfect finish for a rich winter meal.*

*Winter's true saving grace is the desire it arouses
to cook long, slow, comforting dishes. For less money
at this time of year, we can produce dishes of real
substance with complex, intense flavors that are
deeply satisfying.*

Prosciutto with warm chestnuts, arugula, and sage

The combination of warm chestnuts and prosciutto makes a delicious simple winter salad. Fresh chestnuts are fiddly to prepare but well worth the effort, but if you can't be bothered, use good-quality vacuum-packed chestnuts instead.

Serves 4

12 sage leaves

3/4 cup extra virgin olive oil

finely pared zest of 1 lemon, in wide strips

about 30 chestnuts

handful of arugula leaves

12 slices of prosciutto

Start by lightly bruising the sage leaves with a rolling pin or the back of a knife. Place in a small pan with the olive oil and lemon zest over the lowest possible heat. Warm through gently for 10 minutes, then remove from the heat and set aside.

To prepare the chestnuts, make a small, shallow incision on the flatter end of each one with a small knife, then immerse them in a pan of simmering water and cook for 12 minutes. One by one, remove from the pan and peel away the skin using your small knife, while the chestnut is still warm. Place in the warm infused oil.

When all the chestnuts are peeled and added to the oil, return the pan to the lowest possible heat. Warm through gently for about 10 minutes to infuse the chestnuts with the sage and lemon oil. Remove from the heat and set aside for 10 minutes or so, to allow the flavors to adjust to each other.

Just before serving, toss the arugula leaves through the sage-scented chestnuts. Divide the warm chestnut and arugula salad among serving plates. Lay a few slices of prosciutto on top and serve.

Treviso or other radicchio leaves are an excellent

addition to this winter salad. If you have some on hand, simply add a generous handful of roughly torn leaves with the arugula.

Salad of pickled pears, walnuts, bitter leaves, and Gorgonzola

I love to use the young, creamy Gorgonzola cheese, sometimes known as dolcelatte (literally, sweet milk). Its rich, slightly sharp creamy texture works beautifully with walnuts and pears. A perfect warm, wintry salad.

Serves 6

3/4 cup red wine

2 bay leaves

1 small thyme sprig

4 juniper berries

1/4 cup superfine sugar

2 firm, ripe pears (ideally, Comice or Anjou)

1 cup shelled walnuts (preferably, freshly shelled)

large handful of white dandelion leaves or pale frisée

bunch of arugula leaves

7 ounces young Gorgonzola (dolcelatte)

3 tbsp Roasted Red Onions (toolbox, page 29)

1 tbsp minced chervil or curly parsley

Dressing

1 tbsp Dijon mustard

2 tbsp good-quality red wine vinegar

sea salt and freshly ground black pepper

1/3 cup walnut oil

1/3 cup extra virgin olive oil

Pour the wine into a small pan and add the bay leaves, thyme, juniper berries, and sugar. Slowly bring to a simmer over medium heat. Meanwhile, peel, quarter, and core the pears, then cut each quarter in half lengthwise. Add to the pan and poach for 12 minutes, or until just tender. Remove from the heat and let the pears cool in the liquid. Their flavor and beautiful ruby color will intensify as the poaching liquid cools.

In the meantime, shell the walnuts (I gently tap the outside until they crack with a rolling pin). Wash and pat dry the salad greens. Slice the Gorgonzola into long, fine shards.

For the dressing, put the mustard, vinegar, and some salt and pepper in a bowl. Whisk in the walnut oil, followed by the olive oil.

To assemble, dress the salad greens lightly with 1 tbsp or so of the dressing. Pile into the center of each serving plate and arrange the cheese, pears, and roasted red onions attractively around and on top of the leaves. Scatter over the walnuts, sprinkle with chervil, and spoon a little more dressing onto each plate. Serve at once.

Panade of slow-cooked onions with Gruyère

Similar to the various versions of *aquacotta* you come across in Italy, a panade is basically a dish cooked with bread. It is essentially simple food.

Serves 4

4 tbsp unsalted butter

4 yellow onions, peeled and very finely sliced

1¹/2 tsp superfine sugar

sea salt and freshly ground black pepper

¹/4 cup apple brandy

1 bay leaf

4 thyme sprigs

3 cups Chicken Stock (toolbox, page 18)

To serve

4 slices of good-quality white bread

1 clove garlic, halved

4¹/2 ounces Gruyère, grated

handful of parsley leaves, minced (optional)

Melt the butter in a heavy pan over low heat. Add the onions, sprinkle with the sugar, and add a pinch or two of salt. Sweat gently for 20 minutes, until very soft. The onions will deepen in color as the sugar and butter begin to caramelize and their natural sweetness is teased out.

When the onions are very soft, add the brandy and increase the heat to reduce the liquor, cooking off the alcohol. Add the herbs and pour in the stock. Reduce the heat to medium and cook for another 10 minutes, or until the stock has reduced slightly and the flavor is deep and intense. Discard the herbs.

Toast the slices of bread until golden brown on both sides. Rub with the cut garlic clove while still hot and place one slice in each warm soup plate. Ladle over the onions and their broth and sprinkle with the Gruyère. Finish with a grinding of pepper and a sprinkling of parsley. Serve piping hot.

To appreciate the nature of any dish—its subtleties and complexities—you really need to have cooked it several times. It is only then that you will understand its very heart.

Lentil, red pepper, and cumin soup

This simple, honest, filling soup features my favorite pale lentils from Umbria in Italy. You could use Puy lentils if you like, or any other legumes you have on hand—adjusting the liquid and cooking time accordingly. I seem to serve the soup differently every time I make it—sometimes adding a handful of grated Parmesan and a spoonful of sage oil, or stirring a spoonful of tamari into each bowl.

Serves 4

2 tbsp olive oil

1 red onion, peeled and diced

1 leek, washed, trimmed and diced

2 celery stalks, diced

2 carrots, peeled and diced

2 red bell peppers, halved, cored, seeded, and chopped

3 cloves garlic, peeled and chopped

1 tsp cumin seeds, roasted and ground

2 bay leaves

small bunch of lemon thyme (or regular thyme)

1 cup Castelluccio or Puy lentils

4 cups Chicken Stock (toolbox, page 18) or water

sea salt and freshly ground black pepper

To serve

good handful of curly parsley leaves, minced

drizzle of Lemon-Infused Oil (toolbox, page 44), optional

Heat the olive oil in a large pan over medium-low heat. Add the onion, leek, celery, and carrots and sweat gently for 5 minutes, stirring frequently. Add the bell peppers, garlic, cumin seeds, bay leaves, and thyme and continue to sweat for another 5 minutes. By now, the onion, leek, and celery should be translucent.

Add the lentils, pour in the stock, and bring to a simmer. Reduce the heat and cook, uncovered, for about 20 minutes, or until the lentils are tender. Discard the herbs and taste for seasoning—it will most likely need a good pinch of salt and a generous grinding of pepper.

Ladle the soup into warm bowls and scatter over lots of minced parsley. Finish with a drizzle of lemony oil if you like.

Chickpeas with chile, lime, tamarind, and cilantro

This chickpea dish is one of my favorite comfort foods and I have been making it on a regular basis ever since I tasted something similar many years ago. If I am honest, when feeling indulgent, I like it best with steamed basmati rice, liberally seasoned with sea salt and a generous dollop of ghee! It would also work well as a side dish with slow-cooked lamb that is meltingly falling apart.

Serves 4 to 6

2 tbsp unsalted butter

1 tbsp olive oil

2 red onions, peeled and finely sliced

generous bunch of cilantro

3 cloves garlic, peeled and chopped

1 fresh red chile, seeded and finely sliced

1-inch piece fresh gingerroot, peeled and chopped

1 tbsp Roasted Spice Mix (toolbox, page 16)

1 tbsp tamarind water (see below)

4 carrots, peeled and chopped into chunky pieces

2 (14-ounce) cans chopped tomatoes

2 cinnamon sticks

2 1/2 cups cooked or canned chickpeas, drained and rinsed

1/3 cup maple syrup

1/3 cup tamari or soy sauce

juice of 2 or 3 limes, to taste

Melt 1 tbsp of the butter in a medium heavy pan over low heat and heat until foaming. Pour in the olive oil, stir, then add the onions. Sweat gently for 5 minutes until translucent. Meanwhile, wash the cilantro, separate the leaves, and set aside; mince the stems—you need 2 tbsp.

Add the garlic, red chile, ginger, cilantro stems, spice mix, and the tamarind water. Stir for a minute or so, then add the chopped carrots, tomatoes, and cinnamon sticks. Stir well to combine all the ingredients. Put the lid on, turn the heat to low, and cook, stirring occasionally, for 1 hour. By this stage, the tomatoes will have broken down into the sauce, the carrots should be almost tender, and the flavors really comfortable with each other.

Add the chickpeas, maple syrup, and tamari and cook for another 10 minutes or so. Add the remaining 1 tbsp butter and the lime juice and stir well to combine.

Now it's time to taste. You are looking for a really deep, smooth, spicy, sour, salty, and sweet flavor—one that is totally satisfying. If you haven't achieved this, play around a little, pausing to think what might complete the flavor ... perhaps a touch more tamari or a little more maple syrup. Finish by stirring a generous handful of cilantro leaves through.

Tamarind lends a distinctive sour taste, helping to balance out the sweet, salty, and hot flavors so often found in Asian cooking. I buy the whole pod, keep it in a sealed container in the refrigerator, and break off pieces as I need them. To use, the tamarind pieces are soaked in hot water to cover for 20 minutes. The water takes on the tamarind flavor and it is this that you use once it has been strained. Press the tamarind pulp in your strainer to extract as much flavor as possible.

Smoked haddock chowder

This is a wholesome, calm, comforting winter soup. It's really too much as a first course, but it makes a perfect lunch or late night supper—served simply with a salad and bread.

Serves 4 to 6

2¹/4 pounds smoked haddock fillet

4 cups whole milk

6 black peppercorns

2 tbsp unsalted butter

2 slices of thick-cut bacon, trimmed of rind and chopped

1 leek, washed, trimmed, and diced (include a little of the green part)

3 carrots, peeled and diced

3 celery stalks, diced

3 medium potatoes, peeled and chopped

2 lemon thyme sprigs (or regular thyme)

2 bay leaves

sea salt and freshly ground black pepper

¹/3 cup heavy cream

shredded zest of 1 lemon

small handful of curly parsley leaves, minced

Check the fish for any small pinbones. Pour the milk into a wide pan, add the peppercorns, and place over medium heat. Bring to just under a simmer, then add the smoked haddock and remove from the heat. Set aside until the haddock is cooled—the heat of the milk will be enough to gently poach the fish.

Meanwhile, melt the butter in another pan over gentle heat. When it is foaming, add the bacon and cook for 2 to 3 minutes, or until lightly browned. Add the leek, carrots, celery, potatoes, thyme, and bay leaves and season with a little salt and pepper. Cook over low heat for 10 minutes, or until the vegetables begin to soften.

Drain the haddock, reserving the poaching milk. Once the fish is cool, remove the skin and flake the flesh, keeping it in large chunks. Add to the softened vegetables, then strain the milk into the pan (to remove the peppercorns). Turn up the heat very slightly and cook until the potatoes and carrots are tender. It is important that the milk doesn't boil.

Stir in the cream and warm through, then discard the herbs and check the seasoning. Ladle the chowder into warm soup plates and scatter over the lemon zest and minced parsley to serve.

Pan-fried scallops with horseradish cream and winter greens

You can use any winter greens for this salad. I favor white dandelion, ruby chard, and mizuna; a little chervil thrown in is also rather good. The simple horseradish cream has a delicate balance that does not overpower the sweet scallops. It is also good with mackerel and, of course, rare beef. If serving with beef, add another spoonful of horseradish and a little more mustard for an extra kick if you like.

Serves 4

24 sea scallops, cleaned

handful of arugula leaves

handful of white dandelion leaves or pale frisée

handful of mizuna

finely grated zest and juice of 1 lemon

1 tbsp extra virgin olive oil

sea salt and freshly ground black pepper

1 tbsp olive oil

Horseradish cream

generous 3/4 cup crème fraîche

1 tbsp freshly grated horseradish root

1 1/2 tsp Dijon mustard

sea salt

To serve

minced curly parsley

lemon wedges

First, make the horseradish cream (a day in advance if you like). Put the crème fraîche in a bowl and fold in the horseradish and mustard. Season with salt to taste. (If making ahead, cover and refrigerate, but return to room temperature before serving.)

Trim away the tough muscle from the side of each scallop, then set aside at room temperature. Wash the salad greens, dry well, and combine in a bowl. Dress with the lemon zest and juice and the extra virgin olive oil, then divide among four plates or arrange on a large platter.

Place two heavy (ideally, nonstick) skillets over high heat and allow them to get very hot. Season the scallops lightly with salt and pepper. Drizzle 1/2 tbsp olive oil into each skillet.

When the oil begins to smoke, add the scallops, arranging them in a single layer. It is important not to overcrowd the skillet (if you do, the scallops will stew rather than pan-fry), so cook in two batches if necessary. Cook for 1 minute only, then turn (in the same order that you put them into the pan) and cook for the same amount of time on the other side. The scallops should be crunchy and golden on the surface, with a sweet and delicious taste.

As you remove the scallops from the pan, place them on top of the salad greens, adding a dollop of horseradish cream. Sprinkle with minced parsley and serve straight away, with a wedge or two of lemon on the side.

Scallop coral has a delicate flavor. If you are lucky enough to buy scallops in the shell, I suggest you leave the coral attached when you clean them, but you can remove it if you prefer not to eat it.

Salt cod with tomato, fennel, saffron, and aïoli

The base flavors of this dish are reminiscent of a classic French bouillabaisse. They work brilliantly with salt cod, just as they do with the assortment of fish you encounter in a traditional bouillabaisse. The accompanying garlicky aïoli, once stirred in, helps to create a rich and velvety sauce that has a sublime flavor.

Serves 4

1 3/4 pounds salt cod (see below)

1 large or 2 small fennel bulbs

good pinch of saffron threads

5 tbsp olive oil

1 medium yellow onion, peeled and chopped

sea salt and freshly ground black pepper

1 medium leek, washed and sliced (including a little of the green part)

4 cloves garlic, peeled and chopped

4 tbsp dry white wine

2 (14-ounce) cans good-quality Italian plum tomatoes

3 bay leaves

few thyme sprigs

finely peeled zest of 1 orange

3/4 cup Chicken Stock (toolbox, page 18) or water

2 tbsp black olives (ideally, Niçoise or Ligurian)

To serve

Aïoli (toolbox, page 36)

Trim the fennel and cut into 3/4-inch-thick wedges. Scatter the saffron in a Dutch oven or other heavy pot and place over low heat. When the pot is just hot to the touch, add the olive oil and quickly swirl to cover the bottom. Add the onion, fennel, and a generous pinch of salt. Stir, then cover and cook gently for about 10 minutes, stirring occasionally, until the onion is soft and translucent. Add the leek and garlic and cook for a few minutes.

Pour in the wine and allow it to bubble and evaporate slightly. Add the tomatoes, bay leaves, thyme sprigs, orange zest, and a good sprinkling of pepper. Pour in the stock, bring to a simmer, cover, and cook over low heat for 15 minutes, stirring occasionally.

Meanwhile, lightly rinse the salt cod and slice at an angle into 1 1/2-inch-thick pieces. Gently place the salt cod slices in the pot, nestling them among the other ingredients, and add the olives. Bring to a low simmer and cook for 3 minutes, swirling the pot gently once or twice to allow the flavors to get to know each other. Turn off the heat and let stand for a minute or two.

Serve straight away, from the pot, accompanied by the aïoli, a simple green salad, and warm crusty bread to soak up the juices.

To homecure salt cod, ask your fish supplier for a skinned cod fillet. Rinse it under cold running water and gently pat dry, using a clean cloth. Weigh the fish, then lay it on a stainless steel rack, which fits snugly inside a larger pan. Allowing 1 1/2 tbsp good-quality sea salt per 1 pound 2 ounces of fish, season the fillet evenly on both sides, salting the thicker central section more liberally to ensure there is sufficient for curing. Loosely cover the pan with plastic wrap to keep in the smell as far as possible. Let cure in the refrigerator for 3 days, pouring off any liquid and rinsing the bottom of the pan each day. Cod can be homecured for a week, but this shorter curing gives a delicately flavored salt cod that is perfect for this dish. Unlike salt cod that you buy, it does not need soaking before use, just a light rinsing to remove excess salt.

Chinese five spice powder is a mixtur

Tea-smoked quail with Chinese five spice powder and spinach

Tea-smoking is an ideal way to cook small, delicate game birds like quail. I serve them with spinach here, but you could substitute Asian greens, such as bok choy, Chinese broccoli, or water spinach, as this dish has a definite Asian feel. As always when I use spinach, I am referring to the young, small, bright green leaf, also known as pousse.

Serves 4

1 recipe Tea-Smoking Mixture (toolbox, page 20)

2 tbsp Chinese five spice powder

8 quails

10 ounces young, tender spinach leaves

1 tbsp peanut oil

1 tsp toasted sesame oil

1 fresh red chile, seeded and minced

1/2-inch piece fresh gingerroot, peeled and minced

2 cloves garlic, peeled and minced

2 cups Chicken Stock (toolbox, page 18)

1 tbsp fish sauce

1 tsp jaggery or superfine sugar

1 tbsp lime juice, or to taste

Prepare the tea-smoking mixture, then mix in the five spice powder and set up the tea-smoking equipment as described in the toolbox.

Tea-smoke the quails according to the toolbox instructions, cooking them for 10 minutes. Turn off the heat and let the quails stand in the baking pan with the lid on for another 8 minutes.

Meanwhile, prepare the spinach. First, rinse it well under cold running water until you are sure it is clean. (Spinach needs to be washed thoroughly as it can be very dirty.)

Place a large wok over high heat. When it is smoking hot, add the peanut and sesame oils and swirl to coat the bottom. Add the quails and toss for 2 minutes. Lower the heat slightly, add the chile, ginger, and garlic and cook for a minute to release their flavors.

Ladle in the stock, turn the heat to high, and let bubble and reduce slightly. Add the fish sauce and sugar and stir well. Throw in the spinach and allow it to just wilt and fall. The sauce will make it appear beautiful and glossy.

Remove from the heat and finish with a generous squeeze of lime juice. Taste and add a little more if necessary. The sauce should be sweet, pungent, sour, salty, and citrusy—all at the same time! Serve at once.

Szechuan peppercorns, cloves, fennel seeds, star anise, and cinnamon, which you can buy as a mix of whole spices or ready ground. If you take the time to roast and grind your own spices (in equal proportions), your Chinese five spice powder will be infinitely better.

Confit of duck with blood orange and fennel salad

Of all the preserving methods, a good confit maintains the natural flavor of the meat most truly and keeps it succulent. If prepared correctly, the meat is not salty in taste. Confit of duck is best pan-fried or fast-roasted until crispy. Here, I serve it with a simple, yet beautiful blood orange and fennel salad. It works equally as well with a parsnip purée and a simple jus reduction.

Serves 6

1 small bunch of thyme, leaves only, roughly chopped

4 bay leaves, chopped

10 peppercorns, crushed

8 juniper berries, crushed

1½ ounces sea salt

6 duck legs

To confit

4 pounds duck or goose fat (ask your butcher)

¼ bunch of thyme

4 bay leaves

In a small bowl, mix together the thyme, bay leaves, peppercorns, juniper berries, and salt. Scatter half of the mixture over the bottom of a shallow dish. Lay the duck legs side by side and fat side down in the dish, then scatter the remaining mixture over the top. Cover with plastic wrap and refrigerate for 2 days.

Pour off any liquid that has accumulated in the dish, then return to the refrigerator for another 2 days. Remove from the refrigerator and rinse the duck legs under cold running water, then gently pat dry.

To confit, very gently heat the duck fat in a large heavy pan with the thyme and bay leaves. When the duck fat has melted and become translucent, add the duck legs and bring to a low simmer. Turn down the heat and cook very slowly for about 2½ hours. When the skin slips off the shin and the bone is exposed, you know that the duck is ready.

Remove the pan from the heat and let the duck cool in the fat. When completely cool, carefully transfer the duck legs to a very clean earthenware pot. Reheat the fat in the pan, then pour it over the duck legs, making sure they are totally submerged. Let cool, then cover and store in the refrigerator until ready to eat.

"Confit" is an ancient preserving technique—usually applied to duck, rabbit, or pork. To prepare a confit, the meat is first salted and laid down for a few days, then rinsed, dried, and cooked gently in fat. After cooling, the confit can be stored for several months in a sealed container in the refrigerator.

Salad
2 blood oranges
1 fennel bulb
bunch of dandelion leaves
bunch of arugula leaves
small bunch of chervil
bunch of young, tender ruby chard
1 head of treviso or other radicchio

Dressing
juice of 1 blood orange
1 tsp sherry vinegar
1¹/2 tsp Dijon mustard
sea salt and freshly ground black pepper
generous ¹/3 cup walnut oil

When you are ready to eat the confit, carefully remove the duck legs from the fat and set aside to bring to room temperature. Preheat the oven to 500°F (convection oven to 475°F).

For the salad, peel the oranges with a sharp knife, removing all the pith as well as the skin. Slice into fine pinwheels and carefully prize out any seeds. Slice the base off the fennel bulb and remove the fibrous outer layer, then cut the fennel into very fine slices. Wash the salad greens, pat dry, and combine in a salad bowl.

To make the dressing, whisk together the orange juice, vinegar, and mustard in a bowl and season with a little salt and pepper. Whisk in the walnut oil to make a vinaigrette. Taste and adjust the seasoning if necessary.

Place the duck legs, skin side down, in a heavy ovenproof skillet (or sturdy roasting pan) with 2 tbsp of the fat. Warm them gently over low heat until the fat melts, then transfer to the hot oven. Roast until crisp, turning the duck legs once halfway through cooking, 12 to 15 minutes total.

Meanwhile, dress the salad greens lightly with the dressing, then gently toss through the fennel and orange slices. Drain the duck confit on paper towels to absorb any fat. Serve warm, with the blood orange and fennel salad.

Pheasant with beet and roasted tomato purée

Pheasant is a delicious bird. It has a delicate gamey taste that works well with clean, light flavors. The sweet, mellow combination of puréed slow-roasted tomatoes and cooked beets is a perfect match for pan-roasted pheasant breasts. This vibrant purée is equally good with roasted quail, guinea fowl, or chicken. *Illustrated on previous page.*

Serves 4

8 pheasant breasts (with skin)
sea salt and freshly ground black pepper
olive oil

Beet and roast tomato purée

3 large beets, washed
sea salt and freshly ground black pepper
4 Slow-Roasted Tomato halves (toolbox, page 29)
3 tbsp unsalted butter
2 tbsp crème fraîche

To serve

extra virgin olive oil, to drizzle
minced curly parsley

First, make the purée. Put the beets in a pan, add cold water to cover, and season with a little salt. Bring to a boil over high heat, then turn down the heat and simmer until the beets are tender when pierced with a fork—this may take a good 40 minutes. Drain and let the beets cool slightly, then remove the skins and stalks.

Cut the beets into rough cubes and place in a blender, along with the roasted tomatoes, butter, crème fraîche, salt, and a generous grinding of pepper. Blend to a very smooth purée—it will be a beautiful color. Taste and adjust the seasoning if necessary.

Preheat the oven to 425°F (convection oven to 400°F). Season the pheasant breasts all over with salt and pepper. Place an ovenproof skillet over medium-high heat and add a little olive oil. When the pan is hot (almost smoking), add the pheasant breasts, skin side down, and cook for 3 minutes, without moving, until the skin is golden brown. Transfer the skillet to the oven and cook for another 3 minutes (still without turning the pheasant).

Remove from the oven and let the pheasant rest in a warm place for about 10 minutes. Meanwhile, gently reheat the beet and tomato purée in a pan over low heat, stirring to prevent it from sticking or burning.

To serve, divide the warm purée among warm plates and lay the pheasant breasts on top. Drizzle with a little extra virgin olive oil and scatter a little minced parsley over.

Pan-fried veal chops with rosemary and almond aïoli

I love the simplicity of this dish. Veal chops are merely seasoned, pan-fried to a golden, crunchy crust, and served with a punchy rosemary and almond aïoli and wedges of lemon. Plainly cooked spinach, drizzled with the best extra virgin olive oil, is the perfect complement to this dish. I also like to serve a simple, well-seasoned tomato salad on the side, again lightly dressed with good olive oil.

Serves 6

6 veal chops, about 3/4 inch thick

extra virgin olive oil, for rubbing

1 tbsp minced tender rosemary leaves

2 tbsp olive oil

sea salt and freshly ground black pepper

juice of 1 lemon

Rosemary and almond aïoli

generous 3/4 cup whole blanched almonds

2 tbsp minced tender rosemary leaves

2 cloves garlic, peeled and finely crushed

3 organic egg yolks

juice of 1 lemon

2 tsp Dijon mustard

sea salt and freshly ground black pepper

generous 3/4 cup extra virgin olive oil

To serve

lemon wedges

First, make the aïoli. Preheat the oven to 375°F (convection oven to 350°F). Scatter the almonds on a baking sheet and warm them in the oven for 3 to 5 minutes (to tease out and enhance their natural flavor).

While the nuts are still warm, whiz them in a blender or pound using a mortar and pestle until coarsely ground. Now follow the basic mayonnaise recipe in the toolbox (page 36), combining the rosemary, garlic, and almonds with the egg yolks, lemon juice, mustard, and seasoning before drizzling in the olive oil.

Rub the veal chops all over with a little extra virgin olive oil and the rosemary. Set aside for 10 minutes to allow the flavors to infuse.

Heat the 2 tbsp olive oil in a large heavy skillet until it is very hot and you can see a faint haze rising from the skillet. Season the chops with a generous pinch of salt and a good grinding of pepper. Add the chops to the skillet and pan-fry, without moving, for 6 minutes. Turn the chops and cook for 4 minutes on the other side. Add the lemon juice and scrape up the sediment from the bottom of the skillet to deglaze it.

Serve the veal chops with the pan juices spooned over, accompanied by the aïoli and lemon wedges.

When pan-frying meat, the trick is to season the meat
generously with salt and pepper and to cook it, undisturbed, in a very hot pan. Don't be tempted to prod and turn it every 2 seconds. Leave it alone to develop a deep-colored, slightly salty, crunchy crust on the outside and the meat will be meltingly tender in the center. A good squeeze of lemon juice is the perfect counterbalance to a salty crust.

Braised oxtail with ginger, five spice, and garlic

I love slow-cooking cheaper cuts of meat and oxtail has a fantastic ability to absorb the wonderful aromatic flavors in this recipe. The result is a sticky, fragrant, and beautifully rich meat dish that literally melts in your mouth. A sweet potato purée (see page 182) works well with this dish or, if you want something a little gentler, steamed rice would be perfect.

Serves 3 to 4

2¹/4 pounds oxtail, cut into large pieces

1 tbsp vegetable oil

3 red onions, peeled and finely sliced

1-inch piece fresh gingerroot, peeled and minced

2 fresh red chiles, seeded and chopped

3 cloves garlic, peeled and chopped

bunch of cilantro

1 tbsp Chinese five spice powder (preferably freshly prepared, see page 215)

2 (14-ounce) cans good-quality chopped tomatoes

4 cups Chicken Stock (toolbox, page 18)

¹/4 cup fish sauce

¹/4 cup tamari or soy sauce

¹/3 cup jaggery or 5 tbsp maple syrup

Put the oxtail into a large pan over high heat, cover with cold water, and bring to a boil. Lower the heat and simmer for 15 minutes, then pour off the water. Rinse the oxtail thoroughly under cold running water and set aside to drain.

Place a large cooking pot or casserole over medium heat and add the oil. When it is hot, add the onions, ginger, chiles, and garlic. Turn down the heat to low and sweat gently for 10 minutes, or until the onions become translucent.

Meanwhile, separate the cilantro leaves from the stems and set aside for garnishing if you like. Mince the stems and add these to the pot along with the five spice powder. Stir and cook for a couple of minutes to release the beautiful aromatic flavors.

Add the tomatoes and stock and bring to a gentle simmer, then return the oxtail to the pot, ensuring that the pieces are fully submerged. Braise very gently for 1¹/2 hours, or until the oxtail is really soft and sticky.

Add the fish sauce, tamari, and sugar. Turn up the heat just slightly and continue to cook for another 20 minutes or so. Taste and adjust the seasoning and flavors a little if you need to. Serve piping hot, garnished with cilantro leaves if you so wish.

Cook with feeling and intuition. Trust your judgment when
you are balancing the flavors in a dish—you will know what tastes right. And
don't be intimidated by recipes or unfamiliar ingredients. I continue to make
catastrophic mistakes in my cooking, but I enjoy them almost as much as my
successes now, simply because I learn so much from them.

Spicy meatballs with cilantro and sour cherries

Meatballs are one of those crowd-pleasing, homey dishes. Warm and nurturing, to me they are real comfort food. I often serve these spicy meatballs with a purée of sweet potato, but they are equally good with steaming soft, buttery polenta ... perhaps even better! You will need a generous bunch of cilantro—the stems for the meatballs and sauce, some of the leaves for garnishing.

Serves 4 to 6

Meatballs

13/4 cups ground pork

3/4 cup ground beef

1½ cups fresh white bread crumbs

1 tbsp Roasted Spice Mix (toolbox, page 16)

2 tbsp minced cilantro stems

1 fresh red chile, seeded and minced

2 cloves garlic, peeled and minced

grated zest of 1 lemon

sea salt and freshly ground black pepper

1 tbsp olive oil

To prepare the meatballs, put the pork and beef into a large bowl and add the bread crumbs, spice mix, cilantro, chile, garlic, and lemon zest. Mix together well, using your hands, until evenly blended, seasoning with a good pinch of salt and a grinding of pepper. Form the mixture into small balls, about 1½ inches in diameter.

Heat the olive oil in a wide, deep sauté pan over medium-high heat, then add the meatballs in a single layer (cooking them in batches if necessary to avoid overcrowding the pan). Turn down the heat slightly and pan-fry until the meatballs are nicely browned underneath, then turn and continue to cook until they are well browned on all sides. When the meatballs are evenly colored, remove and drain on paper towels.

To make the sauce, pour off any excess fat from the pan and add the onions. Sweat gently over low heat for 5 minutes, or until they are translucent, then add the cilantro, chiles, ginger, and spice mix. Stir and cook for a couple of minutes, then add the lime juice, followed by the tomatoes, garlic, and a good pinch of salt.

Bring to a simmer, cover, and cook over low heat for 20 minutes, stirring from time to time, until you have a rich, homogenized sauce. Now, add the maple syrup, tamari, and sour cherries and turn up the heat for a moment or two—to allow the flavors to get to know each other.

Sauce

2 red onions, peeled and finely sliced

2 tbsp minced cilantro stems

2 medium fresh red chiles, finely sliced

1¹/2-inch piece fresh gingerroot, peeled and minced

1 tbsp Roasted Spice Mix (toolbox, page 16)

juice of 1 lime

2 (14-ounce) cans good-quality chopped tomatoes

1 clove garlic, peeled and crushed

sea salt and freshly ground black pepper

2 tbsp maple syrup

2 tbsp tamari or soy sauce

scant ¹/2 cup dried sour cherries or dried cranberries

To finish

small handful of cilantro leaves

Add the meatballs to the sauce, lower the heat, and simmer gently for about 20 minutes, until they are cooked through. Remove the meatballs with a slotted spoon to a warm serving dish and keep warm while you make any final adjustments to the sauce.

Taste and assess what is needed—perhaps a little more tamari or maple syrup, or a squeeze of lime juice. What you are looking for is a richly flavored, distinctly Middle-Eastern flavor ... warm, spicy, a little sweet, salty, and sour all at the same time. When you achieve the right balance, pour the sauce over the meatballs and serve, scattered with roughly torn cilantro leaves.

Slow-cooked pork belly with cinnamon, cloves, ginger, and star anise

This is a deliciously rich and unctuous winter dish. I like to serve it with braised lentils, but it is also very good with lightly cooked Asian greens, such as bok choy. You will need to order the pork belly with the rib bones intact.

Serves 6

4 1/2-pound piece organic pork belly (with the ribs intact)

2 cinnamon sticks

3 star anise

1 tsp cloves

1 fresh red chile

1 1/4-inch piece fresh gingerroot, peeled

6 cloves garlic, peeled

2 tbsp chopped cilantro stems

generous 1/3 cup tamari or soy sauce

5 tbsp maple syrup

sea salt and freshly ground black pepper

1 tbsp vegetable oil

To serve

Braised Lentils (toolbox, page 22)

Put the pork belly into a large cooking pot (or pan) in which it fits quite snugly and add cold water to cover. Bring to a boil, then immediately turn off the heat and remove the pork from the pan. Drain off the water and rinse out the pan.

Fill the pan one-third full with cold water and place over medium heat. Add the pork, this time along with the spices, chile, ginger, garlic, and cilantro. If there isn't enough liquid to cover the meat, add some more water. Bring to a boil, then turn down the heat and simmer very gently for 1 1/2 hours, until the meat is cooked and very tender. If you have the rib end, the meat will have shrunk back to expose the tips of the bone. With a pair of tongs, carefully remove the meat from the pan and set aside.

Turn up the heat under the pan to high and add the tamari and maple syrup. (If you don't want the sauce to taste "hot," remove the ginger and chile at this point.) Let the liquid bubble until reduced by half—this will take about 20 minutes. As the sauce reduces, the flavors will become very intense, forming a rich, dark sauce.

In the meantime, slice the pork into individual servings—one rib should be enough per person. Season the ribs with a little salt and pepper. Place a heavy skillet over high heat and add the oil. Heat until the pan is starting to smoke, then add the pork ribs and brown well on both sides until crunchy and golden brown on the surface. Strain the reduced liquor.

To serve, lay a rib on each warm plate (or soup plate) and spoon over the reduced sauce and warm braised lentils. Serve at once.

All oils need to be looked after properly. They don't like heat or too much light because they are easily oxidized and spoiled. Keep the bottles sealed—in a cool, dark cupboard, not right next to the stove. This applies to all oils, including flavored oils, nut oils, and, of course, good-quality extra virgin olive oil— a valuable commodity.

Sautéed savoy cabbage with chile and garlic oils

Savoy cabbage is a lovely, vibrant winter vegetable that works well with slow-cooked dishes and vegetable purées, as well as simple broiled white fish.

Serves 4

1 medium savoy cabbage

sea salt and freshly ground black pepper

1 tbsp Chile Oil (toolbox, page 44)

1 tbsp Garlic Oil (toolbox, page 44)

finely grated zest of 1 lemon

1¹/2 tbsp minced curly parsley

To finish

1 medium fresh red chile, finely shredded

or

a squeeze of lemon juice to taste, plus 1 tbsp minced curly parsley

Remove any damaged outer leaves from the cabbage, retaining those that you can as the dark outer leaves are beautiful when cooked. With a sharp knife, remove the fibrous central core of the outer leaves and then slice the leaves crosswise into fine ribbons. Slice the rest of the cabbage in half lengthwise and similarly cut into ribbons (there is no need to remove the core as it is quite tender).

Bring a large pan of water to a boil over high heat and add a very generous pinch of salt. Plunge the cabbage into the boiling water and allow to just return to a boil. Immediately tip the cabbage into a colander and drain well, then place in a warm bowl.

Drizzle the chile and garlic oils over the cabbage and add the lemon zest and minced parsley. Toss to mix, then taste and add a little seasoning if needed. For an extra kick, scatter over some shredded red chile. Alternatively, add a generous squeeze of lemon juice and sprinkle with minced parsley and a good grinding of pepper. Serve straight away, while piping hot!

Parsnip purée with thyme, mustard, and crème fraîche

Sweet and nutty in flavor, this is a lovely winter purée. It works well with simple broiled meats and with slow-cooked rabbit and chicken dishes.

Serves 4

2¹/4 pounds parsnips, peeled and roughly chopped

sea salt and freshly ground black pepper

4 thyme sprigs

1 tbsp Dijon mustard

4 tbsp unsalted butter

2 tbsp crème fraîche

pinch of freshly grated nutmeg

Place the parsnips in a pan, cover with cold water, and add a good pinch of salt and the thyme sprigs. Bring to a boil over medium heat, then turn down the heat and simmer for 15 minutes, until the parsnips are very tender when pierced with a fork. Remove from the heat and drain in a colander. Discard the thyme sprigs.

Tip the hot parsnips into a blender and add the mustard, butter, crème fraîche, and nutmeg. Whiz to a smooth purée. Check for seasoning—you'll probably need to add a little salt and a generous grinding of pepper. If the purée needs to be warmed through, return to the pan and stir over low heat to reheat before serving.

Blood orange and rosemary gelatin

A lovely, light, palate-cleansing dessert, this is gelatin as it should be—wobbly, cool, and not too sweet. Blood oranges are one of my favorite things. These beautiful, blackberry-scented jewels are usually around from December to March, but they are at their best during January and February— just when winter seems almost too barren to bear. You will need about ten oranges to obtain the amount of juice you need, depending on their size. As the flesh of blood oranges varies in color and pattern, so will the depth of color of this gelatin.

Serves 4

2¹/2 cups freshly squeezed blood orange juice

¹/2 cup superfine sugar

3 rosemary sprigs

3¹/2 sheets of leaf gelatin (or scant 4 tsp powdered gelatin), see toolbox, page 246

sunflower-seed (or other neutral-flavored) oil, to oil

To serve

blood orange slices and a little freshly squeezed juice

Put the orange juice and sugar into a pan. Lay the rosemary sprigs on a cutting board and bruise to release their flavor by pressing them firmly with the handle of your knife, then add to the pan. Immerse the gelatin sheets in a bowl of cold water and let soften for about 5 minutes.

In the meantime, place the pan over gentle heat to dissolve the sugar. As the juice begins to warm through, it will take on the flavor of the rosemary. When the sugar has completely dissolved and the juice comes just to a boil, remove from the heat. Remove the gelatin from the cold water and squeeze out the excess liquid, then add to the hot orange juice and stir to dissolve. Strain through a strainer into a bowl, to remove any pithy bits and the rosemary.

Lightly oil 4 individual ramekins or custard cups, ²/3-cup capacity, and pour in the gelatin. Let cool completely, then place in the refrigerator to set—this will only take 1 or 2 hours. I like to serve these jellies on the day they are made, as they continue to set if you leave them in the refrigerator for longer and can become too firm.

To serve, place a slice of blood orange on each serving plate and squeeze over a little more juice. To unmold each gelatin, briefly dip the base of the mold into warm water, then run a little knife around the rim and invert onto the plate. Serve straight away.

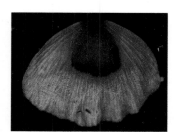

As leaf gelatin varies in potency, you may need to adjust the quantity depending on the brand you are using. My quantity relates to medium-strength gelatin.

Meringues with chestnut purée and cream

When I was nineteen and first moved to Paris, a family friend took me to tea at Angelina's, a beautiful and timeless tearoom on the Rue de Rivoli. I ordered a dessert called Mont Blanc—named after the famous snow-capped mountain—and adored it! Even now, it is still my favorite dessert in the world and I serve it at the restaurant in winter. There is something very old-fashioned and elegant in its taste. The nutty, sludgy taste of the chestnut is the perfect foil for the sticky, sweet meringue. A big dollop of thick cream brings it all together.

Serves 8

Meringue
6 organic egg whites (at room temperature)
pinch of salt
generous 13/4 cups superfine sugar
3/4 tsp vanilla extract

To serve
small can or jar of sweetened chestnut purée
lemon juice (optional)
4 to 6 tbsp thick cream

Preheat the oven to 325°F (convection oven to 300°F). Line a baking sheet with parchment paper. Make the meringue, following the method in the dessert toolbox (page 244). It should be stiff and glossy. Using a large serving spoon, shape 8 generous mounds of meringue on the baking sheet, spacing them well apart to allow room for expansion. Place in the oven and immediately turn down the oven setting to 275°F (convection oven to 250°F). Cook for 45 minutes until crisp. Turn off the heat and let the meringues cool completely in the oven before removing.

Place a meringue in the center of each serving plate. Taste the chestnut purée and add a few drops of lemon juice to counteract the sweetness if necessary. Spoon the cream on top of the meringue and allow it to flow down onto the plate. Place a generous dollop of chestnut purée on top and serve.

The trick is to use a chestnut purée that is not too sweet, so search out a good-quality brand that is not overly sweetened. At the restaurant, we often make our own purée, but it is labor intensive and not necessary here.

Chocolate "tart"

This is really a rich, bitter, grown-up chocolate mousse that I bake in a tart pan. It is essential to use a good-quality chocolate, such as Valrhona. Blood orange slices are a perfect complement; otherwise, a dollop of crème fraîche will suffice. This is a dessert that needs to be served chilled.

Serves 10

butter, to grease

10 ounces good-quality dark chocolate (minimum 64% cocoa solids)

scant 2¹/2 cups heavy cream

6 organic egg yolks

generous 3/4 cup superfine sugar

Preheat the oven to 300°F (convection oven to 275°F). Butter a 10-inch tart pan. Break up the chocolate into small pieces and place in a heatproof bowl over a small pan of simmering water, making sure the bowl isn't in contact with the water. Allow the chocolate to melt on its own, without stirring. Once melted, remove from the heat and slowly stir in the cream to combine. Let cool slightly.

Put the egg yolks and sugar in a separate bowl and whisk for 5 minutes, until the mixture is pale and doubled in volume. Slowly pour the melted chocolate onto the whisked mixture, stirring gently as you do so.

Place the buttered tart pan on a flat baking sheet (to make it easier to negotiate in and out of the oven). Pour in the chocolate mixture and bake until lightly set, 30 to 40 minutes—it will still be a little wobbly in the middle.

Carefully remove the tart from the oven and set aside to cool, then chill in the refrigerator for 1 to 2 hours. The consistency should be almost like a set mousse. A thin slice is enough for anyone!

Winter rhubarb ice cream

Winter rhubarb is my favorite kind. Its beautiful, pale color and bitter, limey yellow leaves are lovely to behold. Cooked gently in a little verjuice or water with a spoonful or two of sugar and a vanilla bean, the tender, pink stalks taste wonderful. They also make a delicious ice cream. *Illustrated overleaf.*

Serves 10

Ice cream base
scant 2 cups heavy cream
2/3 cup whole milk
1 vanilla bean, split lengthwise
6 organic egg yolks
scant 2/3 cup superfine sugar

Rhubarb flavoring
2 1/4 pounds rhubarb
1 vanilla bean, split lengthwise
scant 1 cup superfine sugar
generous 1 cup verjuice (see page 81) or water

Start by making the custard base for the ice cream, following the method in the dessert toolbox (page 248). Set aside to cool.

Wash and trim the rhubarb, then cut into 2-inch chunks. Place in a pan with the vanilla bean, sugar, and verjuice or water. Place over medium-low heat and stir gently, just to start the rhubarb off. Bring to a simmer, then turn down the heat and cook very gently for about 10 minutes, stirring occasionally. The rhubarb should be soft, but not completely falling apart.

Using a slotted spoon, transfer the rhubarb to a bowl. Turn up the heat under the pan and let the liquor bubble until reduced by half. (Rhubarb gives off a lot of liquid during cooking—reducing it down intensifies the flavor.) The reduced liquor should be sharp and sweet at the same time. Pour it over the rhubarb and let cool.

Once the ice cream base has cooled completely, pour it into your ice-cream maker and churn until thickened, according to the manufacturer's instructions. Just before the ice cream sets, pour in the cool rhubarb and churn for another 10 minutes before serving.

The ice cream will be soft and the color will be the most beautiful pale, icy winter pink. Spoon into chilled bowls and serve just as it is … to fully appreciate its wonderful flavor.

DESSERT
TOOLBOX

The basic recipes and techniques in this section enable you to create many different desserts.
Like the main toolbox, the idea of each component is to take one recipe or technique and
master it, so you then have the freedom to take it with you through the seasons. I favor simple
fruit-based desserts, palate-cleansing sorbets and ice creams, and fresh fruit gelatins—light as
air desserts that don't sit heavily after a main course, but leave you feeling revived and refreshed.

Pie dough

This is the recipe I invariably turn to whenever I need a pastry base and it has been a toolbox standby for the past twenty years or so! It is very easy ... but then most things are with practice. Technically, it is a pâte sucrée or sweet pie dough, though I have been known to omit the sugar and add thyme, lemon zest, or grated Parmesan to use it as the base for a savory tart.

for the dough

1 pound 2 ounces all-purpose flour

pinch of sea salt

generous 1 cup unsalted butter, chilled and diced into small cubes

1/4 cup superfine sugar

1 tsp pure vanilla extract

finely grated zest of 1 lemon

1 organic egg, plus 1 egg yolk

5 1/2 tbsp ice water

Sift the flour and salt into a mound on a cool surface. Scatter the butter, sugar, vanilla, and lemon zest over the flour, then toss the ingredients together using a knife or pastry scraper. Make a hollow in the middle and add the whole egg, yolk, and water and toss again.

Gather the dough close to you and, with the heel of your hand, work it away in a quick movement. Keep bringing the dough back to you and working it until it is evenly combined. (Don't worry if little bits of butter show through, it is important not to overwork the dough.)

Once the dough has come together, continue to knead for a minute or so, very lightly. Wrap the dough in waxed paper and chill for 20 minutes (no longer or it will be too difficult to roll out).

Rolling out and making a tart shell

Dust a rolling pin and your surface lightly with flour. Unwrap the dough, place on the floured surface and start to roll. When the dough ball has become a flat circular disk, lift and turn it 90 degrees. Dust with flour and continue to roll, turning it from time to time, until the dough is 1/4 inch thick and the desired shape.

Lay the rolling pin on the edge of the dough and roll the dough around it. Gently lift over the tart pan, then unroll the dough, allowing it to fall loosely over the pan. With your fingertips, lightly press the dough into the sides and bottom of the pan. With a sharp knife, trim away the extra dough overhanging the rim. Prick the base all over with a fork and chill the tart shell for 25 to 30 minutes before baking to prevent shrinking during cooking.

To bake blind (i.e., before filling), line the tart shell with waxed paper and dried beans and bake, following the guidelines in individual recipes.

Pie dough tips

Always use fine-quality ingredients—good unsalted butter, very fresh organic eggs, and pure vanilla extract, not synthetic vanilla essence.

Work quickly on a cold surface—marble is ideal.

Rest the dough twice in the refrigerator (before and after shaping). This helps to prevent shrinking during cooking.

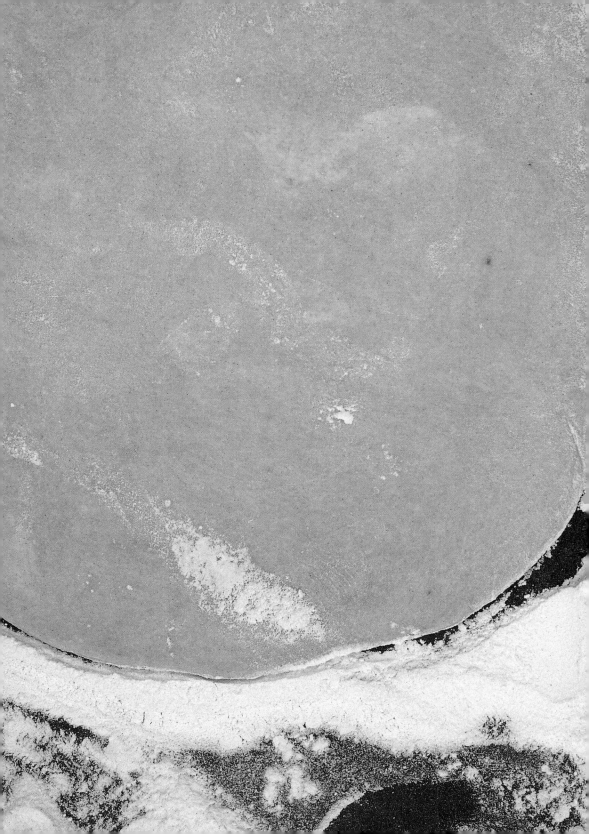

Meringue

I find almost everyone likes meringues. They feel timeless and homey—not like restaurant food at all in my mind. Meringues can, however, be temperamental and need to be treated with respect. They don't like moisture, so they are best cooked in an oven on their own. They also react badly to a sudden change of temperature and are therefore better left to cool completely in the oven, otherwise they are liable to crack. To increase this basic quantity, all you have to remember is to allow a scant 1/3 cup sugar per egg white.

for the meringue

4 organic egg whites (at room temperature)
pinch of salt
1 1/3 cups superfine sugar
1/2 tsp vanilla extract

Preheat the oven to 325°F (convection oven to 300°F). Line a baking sheet with parchment paper. Put the egg whites in a clean, dry bowl and add the salt (this will help to break down the whites). Using an electric mixer or a balloon whisk, beat the egg whites, slowly at first, until they break down and begin to froth a little. Increase the speed and beat until stiff peaks form (that stay upright without flopping at all). Add the superfine sugar, a spoonful at a time, beating all the while. Finally, beat in the vanilla extract. The meringue should be stiff and beautifully glossy.

Place generous spoonfuls of meringue on the prepared baking sheet, spacing them evenly apart to allow room for them to expand. Place in the oven and immediately turn down the oven setting to 275°F (convection oven to 250°F). Cook for 45 minutes, until crisp. Turn off the heat and let the meringues cool completely in the oven before removing. Store the meringues in an airtight container lined with waxed paper for up to 3 days.

Gelatin

l love the pure, palate-cleansing desserts that gelatin enables me to produce. Citrusy fruit gelatins and panna cotta, for example, taste wonderfully light and fresh—the perfect finish to a meal. I prefer to work with leaf gelatin as it lends a beautiful texture and is very satisfactory to work with. Some grocery stores stock it, though I concede it is a lot easier to get hold of powdered gelatin. Use whichever you prefer.

Desserts made with gelatin will continue to firm up the longer they stay in the refrigerator, so don't leave them in for too long: 2 to 3 hours seems to me to be the ideal setting time. When you serve them, they should be wibbly wobbly, not overly firm.

Turning out a dessert

To unmold a gelatin-set dessert, briefly dip the base of the mold in hot water, making sure it only comes halfway up the side. Invert a plate on top, then hold the plate and mold firmly together and turn over, to unmold the panna cotta or gelatin onto the plate. Serve straight away.

Using leaf gelatin

Leaf gelatins vary significantly in strength, so be guided by the package instructions, regardless of what your recipe may indicate. As a rough guide, you need to allow about 4 sheets of leaf gelatin per 2 to 2 1/2 cups liquid.

Soak gelatin leaves in a bowl of cold water for about 5 minutes to soften before using them. Remove and squeeze out excess water before adding to a mixture.

Always add gelatin to hot (but never boiling) liquid, not the other way around, and stir to ensure it dissolves completely.

Strain the mixture through a fine strainer before pouring into molds and let cool completely before placing in the refrigerator to set. Keep covered with plastic wrap in the refrigerator, to ensure that the taste remains pure.

Using powdered gelatin

The same basic guidelines apply. To dissolve, sprinkle powdered gelatin into hot liquid, stirring to dissolve. Or, to make it easier to dissolve, first soften it in cold water (recipes often suggest you do this). Simply put 4 to 5 tbsp cold water in a bowl, sprinkle on the gelatin, and let soften and become spongy for 5 minutes or so. In general, one 1/4-ounce envelope will set 2 cups liquid, but you should follow the package instructions as not all packets are the same size and not all brands work the same.

Ice cream base

All of my creamy ice creams, whether they be fruit, chocolate, or caramel flavored are based on a simple vanilla custard or crème anglaise. Custard in itself is not difficult to make, but it does require a fair amount of vigilance and care.

The custard needs to be cooked over very gentle heat and stirred continuously in a figure-eight movement so that it doesn't stick to the bottom of the pan. Patience is also required to obtain the right consistency—you want to achieve a smooth, velvety custard.

for the ice cream

scant 2 cups heavy cream

2/3 cup whole milk

1 vanilla bean, split lengthwise

6 organic egg yolks

scant 2/3 cup superfine sugar

Pour the cream and milk into a heavy pan and place over low heat. Scrape the vanilla seeds from the bean and add them to the creamy milk with the empty bean pod. Slowly bring to just below a boil, remove from the heat, and set aside to infuse for 15 minutes.

In the meantime, beat together the egg yolks and sugar in a mixing bowl with a whisk, until the mixture becomes thicker and paler. Gently reheat the creamy milk and pour onto the egg yolk mixture, stirring with the whisk as you do so.

Return the custard to the pan and place over the lowest possible heat. Stir gently and patiently until the custard thickens—this will take 6 to 8 minutes (don't be tempted to increase the heat, or you'll have scrambled eggs). It should be thick enough to lightly coat the back of a wooden spoon. Draw a finger along the back of the spoon—it should leave a clear trace.

As soon as the custard thickens, remove from the heat, pour into a bowl, and let cool. Don't leave it in the pan, as the heat of the pan will continue to cook the custard. Once cooled, the custard is ready to strain and use as the base for your ice cream.

Index

The publisher would like to thank Kate
Dyson at the Dining Room store in
Barnes, London, for the loan of crockery
used in some of the photographs.

Acknowledgments

There are so many people I would like to thank. First, my family,
for their enduring love and support, even when I haven't deserved
it, including my brilliant sister, Briony; my brother, David, of
whom I am very proud; much-loved members of my extended
family—Leila, Eliza, Jeremy, Bella, and Ben—and my father, Bruce,
whom I miss dearly. To my mother, Ann, who is profoundly
talented—her mind is like a magic box full of amazing thoughts
and dreams ... I love her very much. And, of course, to my two
beautiful and extraordinary girls, Holly and Evie, and to James,
whom I love and whose love and support have been constant.

To Gael and Francesco Boglione, who had a dream to build
something beautiful and let me come along for the ride. They are
very inspiring to work with, and dear friends.

From the bottom of my heart, I thank everyone I work with at
Petersham, including my wonderful kitchen team—Marlon, Dino,
Fabio, Suzannah, Ismael, Ros, Clare, and others who have come
and gone. Also our front-of-house team, notably Jo, who has been
with us from the start. Special thanks to Rachel Lewis, the best
maître d' I know, and Wendy Fogarty, who organizes all our events
and sources beautiful produce for me to use in the kitchen. Both
are more to me than work colleagues ... they are treasured friends.
I am also grateful to Lucy Boyd, who lovingly tends our kitchen
garden, and to Sarah Canet, whose guidance has been invaluable.
Many have left their mark on Petersham, not least Sophie Cookes,
whose year spent in the kitchen with me was an absolute joy!

Thank you to everyone who has worked so hard on this book,
including Jane O'Shea at Quadrille, who commissioned me in the
first place; Janet Illsley, my lovely, patient, and gentle editor;
Lawrence Morton, for his beautiful design and layout; and Jason
Lowe, whose extraordinary photographs gave me the courage
to go ahead with the book. I am especially grateful to the
wonderful Lisa Campbell, who has been part of our family for the
past six years and who painstakingly typed every single word for
this book ... thank you, Lisa.

Last, I would like to thank all my dedicated producers and
suppliers. And the truly inspirational female chefs I admire so
much, including Alice Walters, Maggie Beer, Stephanie Alexander,
Gay Bilson, Rose Gray, and Judy Rodgers, some of whom I have
had the privilege to work with. Thank you especially to Layla
Sorfie, who was the first to nurture and inspire me!

A FINAL WORD

It was with some trepidation that we purchased the old nursery at the foot of our garden, as we didn't quite know what to do with it. We wanted Petersham Nurseries to be as beautiful as our family home, which we had lovingly restored over five years. So that's how our project began. With the same effort, we set about tossing out the plastic, ripping up the concrete, and banishing pesticides ... all with the aim of moving to a more sustainable environment. After all, that's the way forward, that's the future.

Day by day the nurseries evolved into a magnificent mish-mash of rambling sweet-smelling jasmine, giant tickling ferns, antique zinc tubs filled with dahlias, and rust-spotted urns planted with exquisite miniature roses ... all dotted with weird and wonderful pieces from our travels. In such an environment, it was probably inevitable that the nursery would begin to take on an otherworldly feel and a life of its own, both wistful and optimistically modern.

As the nurseries took shape, it became evident that this would be an enticing environment in which to eat some fabulous food. I immediately thought of Skye, who not only cooks as you cannot imagine, but is a person of extreme passion and integrity. Never in my wildest dreams did I think this greatly experienced and talented woman would offer to run a restaurant from a garden shed, but she did! And that's how Petersham Nurseries Cafe was born ... from passions shared by like-minded souls.

Petersham Nurseries Cafe is the antithesis of the slick city restaurant. Instead of shiny floors and be-suited waiters, we have dirt on the ground and waitresses in wellies. Yet as inauspicious as it sounds, I think we have taken eating and experiencing food to another level. Skye sources incredible produce and her food is very special. Some describe it as simple, but I have seen her agonize over every last detail. She shares her passion with every mouthful. This book is a testament to Skye and her unique style of cooking ... I am so proud of her.

Gael Boglione